The Biography of Stephen Hawking

By Nina Wegner

Level 5

IBC パブリッシング

はじめに

　ラダーシリーズは、「はしご（ladder）」を使って一歩一歩上を目指すように、学習者の実力に合わせ、無理なくステップアップできるよう開発された英文リーダーのシリーズです。

　リーディング力をつけるためには、繰り返したくさん読むこと、いわゆる「多読」がもっとも効果的な学習法であると言われています。多読では、「1.速く 2.訳さず英語のまま 3.なるべく辞書を使わず」に読むことが大切です。スピードを計るなど、速く読むよう心がけましょう（たとえばTOEIC®テストの音声スピードはおよそ1分間に150語です）。そして1語ずつ訳すのではなく、英語を英語のまま理解するくせをつけるようにします。こうして読み続けるうちに語感がついてきて、だんだんと英語が理解できるようになるのです。まずは、ラダーシリーズの中からあなたのレベルに合った本を選び、少しずつ英文に慣れ親しんでください。たくさんの本を手にとるうちに、英文書がすらすら読めるようになってくるはずです。

《本シリーズの特徴》
- 中学校レベルから中級者レベルまで5段階に分かれています。自分に合ったレベルからスタートしてください。
- クラシックから現代文学、ノンフィクション、ビジネスと幅広いジャンルを扱っています。あなたの興味に合わせてタイトルを選べます。
- 巻末のワードリストで、いつでもどこでも単語の意味を確認できます。レベル1、2では、文中の全ての単語が、レベル3以上は中学校レベル外の単語が掲載されています。
- カバーにヘッドホーンマークのついているタイトルは、オーディオ・サポートがあります。ウェブから購入/ダウンロードし、リスニング教材としても併用できます。

《使用語彙について》
レベル1：中学校で学習する単語約1000語
レベル2：レベル1の単語＋使用頻度の高い単語約300語
レベル3：レベル1の単語＋使用頻度の高い単語約600語
レベル4：レベル1の単語＋使用頻度の高い単語約1000語
レベル5：語彙制限なし

Table of Contents

Timeline *2*

Introduction *4*

Childhood and Education *9*

Diagnosis of Motor Neuron Disease *16*

Marriage, Family, and a PhD *22*

Early Research and Discoveries *29*

International Fame and a Brush with Death *42*

Writing *A Brief History of Time* *56*

A Sad Period *60*

Into the 21st Century *68*

Word List *76*

ホーキング・ストーリーを読むにあたって

　理論物理学は、数式を軸とした理論をもって、この世の中、そして宇宙の謎を解き明かしてゆこうとする学問です。

　現在は実験の結果を横目にみながら、それを数値をもって裏付けてゆくのか、あるいは数値をもって推論をたて、それを実験によって証明するのかという物理学の基本的なアプローチを個人がこなすことは不可能な時代です。

　実験の規模も大きくなり、ましてや宇宙を相手に実験をすることなどは不可能です。であればこそ、アインシュタインが相対性理論を発表したように、数学の力を借りながら、実験をするにはあまりにも壮大な宇宙の成り立ちや、そこでおきている現象を解明してゆこうと人々は試みます。それが理論物理学という分野を発展させたのです。

　ホーキングは、ブラックホールのメカニズムを解明し、ブラックホールが素粒子を放出しながら消滅に向かうという理論を打ち立てました。

　理論物理学の世界には、極めて高度な数学への造詣が求められますが、同時にそこで語られる世界は、極めてロマンチックで壮大なSFの世界です。もちろんそれはフィクションではなく、論理をもって宇宙の謎を解明

するという壮大な試みですが、理論物理学で語られるブラックホールの世界や、時空を超えた4次元の世界は、我々の想像力に刺激を与え、SF小説よりもSFらしい、空想の世界に我々を導くのです。

ホーキングは筋萎縮性側索硬化症という難病と闘いながら、奇跡的に生き延びた学者として知られています。彼の理論物理学者としての才能を「無限」とした場合、彼の肉体的なハンディキャップは、無限からそのハンディキャップ分の数値を差し引いたものに過ぎないと、ここで強調します。

つまり、無限からいかに数値を引こうと、また足そうと、無限に変わりはないのです。彼の才能は宇宙という無限と取り組む才能です。このレベルの知性は、肉体的なハンディキャップがあろうとなかろうと、変化するものではないのかもしれません。

ラダーシリーズでホーキングを取り上げたのには理由があります。理論物理学という高度な学問をSFのように楽しみ、同時にサイエンスにからむ表現や語彙を習得するには、まさにホーキングのような人物の伝記に触れるのが一番だからなのです。ぜひホーキングの伝記を通して、英語でサイエンスを語る楽しみを味わってください。

【本書に登場する科学者】

Galileo Galilei（1564-1642）ガリレオ・ガリレイ。イタリアの物理学者・天文学者。自作の望遠鏡で天体観測を行い、地動説を裏付ける証拠を数多く発見し、論文を発表した。地動説とは、地球を中心に天体が動いているのではなく、地球が自転しながら他の惑星とともに太陽の周りを動いているという説で、もともとはコペルニクスが唱えたもの。ガリレオは地動説を支持したために異端審問にかけられ有罪判決を受けた。

Isaac Newton（1642-1727）アイザック・ニュートン。英国の物理学者, 数学者, 自然哲学者。慣性の法則(物体は運動の状態を持続する)、万有引力の法則(あらゆる物質には引き合う力を持つ)を発見した。近代物理学の父と目される人物。ニュートン力学の確立によって、地動説は真理として認められるに至った。

Albert Einstein（1879-1955）アルベルト・アインシュタイン。ドイツ生まれのユダヤ人理論物理学者。相対性理論を発表し、時間は誰にとっても一定であるというそれまでの常識を覆した。20世紀最大の物理学者、現代物理学の父と目される人物。

【本書に登場する科学用語】

Gravity 重力。万有引力。あらゆる物質が持つ互いに引き合う力。重力の強さは物質の質量が大きいほど強くなり、距離が近づくほど強くなる。

Theory of Everything 万物の理論。自然界に存在する四つの力（①電磁気力：電気・磁気に基づく力、②弱い力：素粒子間レベルの非常に近い範囲で作用する

力、③強い力：原子の中心にある原子核同士を結合している力、④重力）の法則をそれぞれに分けて説明するのではなく、すべてまとめて説明することができる理論。物理学者マクスウェルは、別々の現象であると考えられていた電気と磁気とを一つに統合した。

General relativity 一般相対性理論。アインシュタインが見出した時間・空間に関する理論。光が重力によって曲がることや、時間の流れが観測者によって一定ではないといった予測を証明し、それまでの時空に関する常識を覆した。

Black hole ブラックホール。極めて巨大で高密度な天体。強い重力を有するために物質のみならず光も脱出することができず、そのため観測することができない。

Event horizon 事象の地平線。光（光速）でも到達できなくなる領域が宇宙には存在し、その領域の境界のこと。例えばブラックホールは強い重力を持つため、ブラックホールに近づきすぎると光さえもその重力から逃れることができなくなる。この脱出可能領域と、脱出不可能な領域を隔てるポイントを指す。

Big Bang ビッグバン。137億年前に起こった、時空の始まりとされる大爆発。ハッブルがあらゆる銀河が地球から遠ざかっていることを発見して以来、宇宙は膨張し続けていることがわかった。ということは、過去に遡るほど宇宙は収縮してゆき、原初の宇宙は高密度・超高温の火の玉のような存在であったに違いないというビッグバン説が1940年代に唱えられ、現在では標準的宇宙理論として認められている。

The Biography of Stephen Hawking

By Nina Wegner

Timeline

January 8, 1942 – Birth.

1963 – First year at Cambridge. Meets Jane Wilde at a New Year's party before diagnosis. Diagnosed with motor neuron disease. Doctors predict he only has two years to live.

1965 – Marries Jane Wilde.

1966 – Earns a PhD in cosmology.

1967 – Birth of first child, Robert.

1968 – Becomes member of the Institute of Astronomy in Cambridge.

1970 – Birth of second child, Lucy.

1973 – Publishes first book, *The Large Scale Structure of Space-Time*.

1974 – Becomes celebrated in the scientific world with the theory of Hawking radiation.

1979 – Becomes the Lucasian Professor of Mathematics at Cambridge University. Birth of third child, Timothy.

1982 – Starts writing *A Brief History of Time*.

1985 – Loses voice following a tracheotomy and requires 24-hour nursing care. Starts using computer speaking program.

1988 – Publishes *A Brief History of Time*, which becomes an international bestseller.

1990 – Separates from Jane and begins to live with one of his nurses, Elaine Mason.
1992 – Errol Morris makes *A Brief History of Time*, a biographical movie about Stephen.
1995 – Divorces Jane, marries Elaine Mason several months later.
2001 – Publishes *The Universe in a Nutshell* in a continued effort to make cosmology and theoretical physics accessible to the masses.
2003 – Nurses accuse Elaine of physically abusing Stephen, but Stephen denies these claims.
2005 – Publishes *A Briefer History of Time*.
2006 – Divorces Elaine.
2007 – Experiences zero gravity. Publishes *George's Key to the Universe*, a children's science book, with his daughter, Lucy.
2009 – Retires from his position as the Lucasian Professor of Mathematics at Cambridge University.
2010 – Publishes *The Grand Design*.
2014 – The Oscar-nominated movie about his life, *The Theory of Everything*, is released.

Introduction

Have you ever wondered where the universe comes from and where it started? There are many scientists whose full-time job is to think about these things. Stephen Hawking is the most well known of these modern-day scientists.

Stephen Hawking is the world's most famous and popular theoretical physicist alive today. Theoretical physics is the study of nature through the use of mathematics and theoretical models. This branch of physics is very different from other branches, such as quantum physics or experimental physics. As a theoretical physicist, Stephen Hawking does much of his research in his head. His breakthroughs are based on many hours thinking, rather than many hours of experimenting. He does not conduct physical experiments, but instead solves questions about the universe by applying mathematical concepts to them.

Many people believe that Stephen Hawking is one of the greatest thinkers of our time. He has contributed key theories to the debate about how the universe works. Also, for much of his career, Stephen Hawking searched for the "theory of everything" (also known as TOE), one of the biggest unsolved problems in physics. A "theory of everything" would explain how everything in the universe works, bringing all the different branches of physics together under one ruling theory. Currently, the laws of the universe are split into two main theories. These are general relativity and quantum mechanics. General relativity uses the laws of gravity to look at big bodies, such as stars and planets. Quantum mechanics, on the other hand, uses the law of thermodynamics to look at very small bodies, such as atoms. Although these two theories both work in their separate fields, they can't both be right when applied to the same problems. This is where the "theory of everything" comes in. A theory of everything would be one law that works every time, when applied to anything in the universe. Many scientists and physicists think the discovery of a theory of everything would be humanity's most important discovery.

Stephen Hawking has devoted much of his life to finding the theory of everything. Although he has not found it yet, he has provided new ideas and theories that have brought the field of physics closer to discovering a theory of everything.

Stephen's strength of mind, however, is coupled with a weakness of the body. He was diagnosed with motor neuron disease (also known as Lou Gehrig's Disease and amyotrophic lateral sclerosis, or ALS) at the young age of twenty-one. He has overcome enormous hardships and physical disability to become one of the world's leading thinkers. It is commonly thought that he is also the world's most famous disabled person.

Stephen's many breakthroughs in math and science has won him many high honors and awards from all around the world. Over the years, he has also become an icon in popular culture and mainstream media. Today, at the age of seventy-four, Hawking continues to

Stephen Hawking and his daughter Lucy Hawking.

think about some of the biggest questions in science, such as how the universe was created and the true nature of time. He also continues to make these difficult topics accessible to the general public.

Childhood and Education

Stephen William Hawking was born on January 8, 1942, during the height of World War II. He was born in Oxford, England, to parents Isobel and Frank Hawking. Isobel and Frank were living in North London when Isobel became pregnant with Stephen. But because London was under constant danger from nightly air raids, she went to Oxford to give birth. Here, in the safer and quieter surroundings of the old college town, she had their first child, Stephen.

Isobel and Frank were not wealthy, but

they were very intelligent people who valued education. Frank was a doctor who specialized in tropical diseases. Isobel had studied philosophy, politics, and economy at Oxford University. She graduated from Oxford in the 1930s, a time when few women attended university, let alone one of the country's most prestigious ones.

Stephen grew up in a three-story brick house in the town of St. Albans, just east of Oxford and north of London. He had two sisters, Mary and Philippa, and an adopted younger brother, Edward. Mary was just eighteen months younger than Stephen, and Philippa was five years younger than him. Edward was adopted when Stephen was fourteen years old.

As a child, Stephen was active and bright, but was not always at the top of his class. He was slow in learning to read, which he has blamed on the "progressive style" of his early education. He was known to have terrible handwriting. But Stephen was very clever and interested in how things worked, such as clocks and radios. He was always asking "how" and "why" questions. Much later in his life, Stephen said that he is still "just a child who has never grown up. I still keep asking these how and why questions. Occasionally I find an answer."

School and studies did not interest Stephen as much as games. One of his favorite games as a youngster was to find different ways of climbing into the family's house with his sister Mary. He also loved board games, and he and his friends often created their own. They were usually large and complicated games that reproduced entire systems, such as industry, feudalism, and stock markets. In his autobiography, Stephen described these games as an early "urge to understand how systems worked and how to control them." He was later able to satisfy his desire for control through his studies at university. He commented, "Since I began my PhD, this need has been met by my research into cosmology.

If you understand how the universe operates, you control it, in a way."

Although Frank Hawking, Stephen's father, wanted his son to follow in his footsteps as a doctor, Isobel saw that Stephen was more interested in stars than medicine. When the weather was nice, the family often gathered in the yard to look at the stars together. During these times, she noticed how curious Stephen was about the night sky. Later, Stephen would find great pride in having been born on the three-hundredth anniversary of Galileo's death. Galileo was a great astronomer and is considered the father of modern science. This has become a meaningful coincidence for Stephen.

Neighbors and friends described the Hawkings as a unique family. They didn't seem to fit with the way other families did things, both in the home or out in society. For example, the family car was an old London taxi. To give the children something fun to play with, Frank and Isobel bought an old

Childhood and Education

gypsy caravan, which they kept in the yard. The children played in the caravan much like it was their clubhouse. Dinnertime at the Hawkings' house was not necessarily a time for family bonding. According to one family friend, meals at the Hawking home were usually eaten in total silence because each member of the family would be reading a book. The Hawkings also treated their home as a laboratory, where they kept bees and made fireworks.

When Stephen was seventeen years old, he enrolled at University College at Oxford, in 1959. He wanted to study mathematics, but his father discouraged him to get a degree in that subject. Listening to his father, Stephen turned to physics instead. This is when he began to explore the world of cosmology.

Stephen later admitted that up until this time, he had not put much time or effort into his studies at school. He estimated that he spent only about an hour each day studying. He also said he found his coursework to be easy and boring. However, this would soon change once the difficult questions of how the universe works began to spark his imagination and challenge his intellect.

Stephen Hawking graduated from the Oxford University with honors in natural science in 1962. He went on to continue his graduate studies at Cambridge University. He worked and studied under his PhD advisor, British physicist Dennis Sciama. Today, Sciama is considered one of the fathers of modern cosmology.

During this time in history, physics and cosmology circles were involved in a great debate about the origin of the universe. One group believed in the theory of a "Steady State" universe, which says that the universe is expanding but always creating new matter to keep the same amount of density. In essence, this group believed that there was no "beginning" or "end" to the universe; they believed the universe remained the same in appearance at all times. The other group believed in the theory of the "Big Bang," which held that the expanding universe came from the explosion of a very dense, very small point in space-time. Over the years, Stephen Hawking's research would come to play a major role in this debate.

Diagnosis of Motor Neuron Disease

During Stephen's undergraduate years at Oxford, he pursued many interests, including dancing and rowing. He joined the Oxford rowing team and became the team's coxswain—the leader who shouts orders to the rowers. However, during his last year at Oxford, Stephen began to feel clumsy. He found he had trouble doing simple things, and sometimes his body would not move in the way he wanted it to. He had trouble rowing. At one point, he fell down some stairs at school and hit his head. He also noticed moments of slurred speech. However, he ignored these incidents until one year, when he was at home for Christmas, his family also noticed his troubles. Worried, they asked him to go to the hospital. Finally, in 1963, during his first year at Cambridge, Hawking went to see the doctor. A long, unpleasant process of testing began.

At the hospital, doctors stuck electrodes onto Stephen to study his muscle movement. They cut into his arm to take a muscle sample. They even injected his spine with a special fluid to read its movement through X-rays. At first, they were not able to diagnose him properly—the most they could do was rule out multiple sclerosis.

These tests continued for two weeks, making Stephen quite miserable. Finally, the doctors were able to diagnose the problem. Stephen and his family were told that he was showing early symptoms of motor neuron disease, or amyotrophic lateral sclerosis (ALS), also known as Lou Gehrig's disease. Motor neuron disease is a neurological disorder in which the nerves that control muscles shut down. This results in shrinking muscles. Due to the shrinking muscles, people with motor neuron disease lose their movement, including the ability to walk, talk, swallow, and even breathe.

Among patients of motor neuron disease, Stephen was a rare case. His particular form of the disease was early-onset. While most people with motor neuron disease begin to show symptoms later in life, at around fifty or sixty years old, Stephen was diagnosed at age twenty-one. With heavy hearts, his doctors told him that he had roughly two years to live.

Hearing this awful news, Stephen could have easily given up his desire to live. In fact, he fell into a deep depression for a while. However, several events that occurred around this time gave Stephen the motivation to keep fighting for his life. In the end, this motivation may have helped him become the brilliant scientist and thinker he is now.

While Stephen was in the hospital undergoing the tests, he shared a room with a boy who was suffering from leukemia. The boy died, giving Stephen new perspective. Every day, he saw what this young person had to go through because of his illness, and Stephen decided that perhaps his own situation was not so bad. Later, after he was released from the hospital, he had a dream that convinced him he still had work to do. In the dream, he saw himself being executed. This sparked a new will in him to make the most of his life while he had the chance.

But, perhaps most importantly, Stephen had recently met a girl. In 1963, roughly a month before he was diagnosed with motor neuron disease, he had met Jane Wilde, an eighteen-year-old student at Westfield College in London, a women's school. Jane was a slender, dark-haired, shy girl with kind eyes. She was also from St. Albans. She remembered going to school for a brief while with the Hawking sisters. She also remembered seeing

Stephen walking down a street of St. Albans one day in the summer of 1962. She later said that his mop of messy brown hair, his thick glasses, and his clumsy way of walking had made a strong impression on her. She was surprised to hear that her good friend Diana King had once gone on a date with Stephen. She also discovered that Stephen was Diana's brother's friend.

Diana invited Jane to a New Year's party that she and her brother, Basil, threw on New Year's Day, 1963. Jane attended the party wearing a green dress. And there, talking with a friend, she saw Stephen Hawking, dressed in a black coat and red bowtie. That day, Jane and Stephen formally met and exchanged contact information.

Shortly afterward, Stephen invited Jane to his twenty-first birthday party at his family's house. Although they didn't say much to each other, Jane's admiration of Stephen's cleverness and unique personality grew. One afternoon, they met on a train when Stephen was heading back to Cambridge, and he told her he often came home on weekends. He asked her if she'd like to go to the theater sometime. She accepted.

After their first date, a trip to the theater, Stephen invited Jane to the May Ball at Cambridge. But by the time of the ball, which took place in summer, Stephen's health had declined noticeably. As the months went by, the couple found themselves falling in love, but both questioned their future together with Stephen's illness progressing. The doctors had given him only two years to live, and this cast a shadow on the young couple's hopes and plans. However, Stephen refused to talk about his illness with Jane, almost as if he thought talking about such things would cast a curse on his life and his new relationship.

Marriage, Family, and a PhD

One Saturday evening in the autumn of 1964, Stephen Hawking proposed to Jane Wilde. She happily accepted. Her father made the couple promise that Jane would finish her studies at university despite becoming a married woman. Stephen and Jane promised, and both the Hawking and Wilde families welcomed the wedding.

During this time, Stephen still struggled with his illness and the prognosis that his doctors had given him. Perhaps the thought of only having two years made him more outspoken and opinionated than he already was. At parties and gatherings, he would announce his controversial political beliefs to whoever would listen. He also argued with people about any topic. This often embarrassed Jane, but the two continued to get along. They hoped to make the most of whatever time they had together. Stephen would excitedly call Jane at her London apartment, and together they would talk about their wedding and their plans for the future. But, they faced another problem: before they could marry, Stephen had to find a way of providing housing and an income for him and Jane.

Stephen had applied to research astronomy under Professor Fred Hoyle at Cambridge, a brilliant and famous British scientist who was well known from his frequent television appearances. However, Hoyle had rejected Stephen's application and Stephen was assigned to study under Dennis Sciama. However, Hoyle entered Stephen's life in another way that brought Stephen much attention in the scientific circle. In June of 1964, the third year of Stephen's graduate studies, Stephen attended a talk on the theory of the steady-state universe that Hoyle had researched with two other scientists. After the talk, Stephen rose from his seat in the audience and told Hoyle that his calculations were wrong. When Hoyle asked Stephen how he knew, Stephen replied that he'd simply worked out the calculations in his head.

This shocking statement made the scientific circle notice Stephen Hawking. It was also around this time that Stephen began to collaborate with British mathematician Roger Penrose, who was working on a mathematical model of the theory of singularity and gravitational collapse. The theory argued that once a star's gravity had forced it to collapse in on itself, it became a "singularity," or a point in space-time where the laws of relativity stopped working. Penrose believed that this singularity existed in a space that would later be named a "black hole." Stephen built on this theory and applied it to the entire universe. He proposed that reversing these same mathematical calculations would prove that the expanding universe necessarily came from just such a singularity. This idea later became the basis for the Big Bang Theory. Already, Stephen was starting to form ideas that would change the way we understand the origin the universe.

This topic—the way expanding universes worked—became the basis of Stephen's PhD research. He set to work applying for prizes and research fellowships to both farther his career and to provide some income for himself and his fiancée.

In early 1965, Stephen Hawking was awarded a Gonville and Caius Research Fellowship in cosmology at the University of Cambridge. The fellowship was very prestigious and ensured a salary for Stephen and Jane to live on. Thrilled with this news, the couple officially set the date of their wedding for July 14, 1965.

Stephen and Jane were married in the Trinity Hall Chapel at Cambridge University. After the wedding, the couple spent a relaxing week honeymooning in the beautiful country town of Long Melford in Suffolk County. Driving the old red Mini they had bought with their savings, the couple toured the countryside and stayed at a Tudor-style inn. It was a peaceful and lovely first week of marriage.

Soon after the honeymoon, however, it was back to work. Stephen and Jane flew to Cornell University in New York, where Stephen was attending summer school. There, among the gathering scientists, Stephen discovered something exciting. The physics and cosmology circles in America—not just the UK—recognized his name. They knew about his comments at Hoyle's lecture a year ago, and they knew about his work with Roger Penrose. To his delight, he realized he was becoming an international figure in physics.

But not everything was rosy. As Stephen's fame as a physicist gained strength, his body grew weaker. He could no longer drive a car, and walking took a long time. Jane had to help him with much of his transportation outside of the house. But, Stephen felt there was at least one good result of his weakening body. Many years later, Stephen would note that it was this sense of his time running out that drove him to achieve great scientific breakthroughs.

According to a memoir written by Jane Hawking, Stephen's advisor, Dennis Sciama, said early on that Stephen "had a career of Newtonian proportions ahead of him." This statement turned out to be true in many ways. In March of 1966, Stephen published his doctoral thesis and earned a PhD in cosmology at Trinity College at Cambridge University. His thesis, written in collaboration with Roger Penrose, was called "Singularities and the Geometry of Space-Time." Its publication earned him and Penrose the Adams Prize, a prestigious annual prize given by the Faculty of Mathematics at the Cambridge University.

Stephen provided mathematical evidence for the Big Bang theory and was now being called a brilliant astrophysicist in international science circles.

But just a few months later, by the autumn of 1966, Stephen needed Jane's help to go everywhere. He could not even walk short distances on his own, and his speech was becoming harder for people to understand. He lost motor skills in his hands, and he could not write anymore except to sign his name. It was at such a time that Stephen discovered he was going to be a father.

Robert George Hawking was born at ten o'clock at night on Sunday, May 28, 1967. Stephen was so overcome with emotion over the birth of his first child that when he told his neighbors the news, they thought Jane had died in childbirth. But in fact, both mother and baby were perfectly healthy and Stephen was absolutely filled with joy.

Early Research and Discoveries

After publishing his thesis in 1966, Stephen had an opportunity to travel to the United States again. He attended summer school at the Battelle Memorial Institute in Seattle, Washington, then went on a two-week trip to the University of California, Berkeley. Later, he spent some time at the University of Maryland. Jane and Robert, still a newborn baby, came with him everywhere he went.

At the Seattle summer school, it became clear to everyone that Stephen was a leader in the field of black holes. His research and ideas thrilled the scientists and physicists gathered there. From that point on, Stephen decided to accept any and all opportunities for lectures, conferences, and seminars around the world. As he began to accept international invitations to speak or present his research, his fame grew. And in just a few years, he rocketed to the top levels of astrophysics research. He was becoming a well-known name in the science world.

Of course, there was good reason for his rising fame. Stephen could visualize mathematical models in many dimensions. He also had an incredible memory. In 1968, at just twenty-six years old, Stephen became a member of the new Institute of Astronomy, located just outside of Cambridge. Sadly, however, this was not a paid position and Stephen and Jane worried about what would happen when his two-year research fellowship expired in 1969. Thankfully, Stephen's rising fame worked in his favor. In 1969, Gonville and Caius College at Cambridge University created a special position just to keep Stephen on their faculty. He accepted their offer of a Fellowship for Distinction in Science. It offered a good income and lasted six years. With this job security and a comfortable income for his growing family, Stephen could now continue his research without worry.

In 1970, Stephen and Jane's second child, Lucy, was born. Around this time, Stephen's health declined even further. Although he had resisted for years, he was now forced to use a wheelchair. However, he still insisted on

Stephen Hawking and his son.

doing as much for himself as he could. This included undressing himself every night before bed. According to Jane's memoirs, this nightly routine was a difficult and slow process for Stephen, but he kept at it. Once Jane had undone his shoelaces and buttons, Stephen would get out of his clothes and put on his pajamas. As he struggled with his clothes and the minutes ticked by, he would think about his questions of the universe.

One evening, as he undressed himself, he was able to solve a major problem about the surface area of black holes. Astrophysicists at the time had been struggling with the question but no one had come up with the answer. Changing into his pajamas, Stephen solved the problem. He mathematically deduced that the event horizon (or the point where gravity becomes so great that nothing can escape) of a black hole could never get smaller. This came to be known as the second law of black hole dynamics. This was a remarkable discovery at the time, especially for someone so young:

Stephen was only twenty-eight years old. It was only years later that Stephen would replace this law himself with a further discovery that black holes do radiate particles, proving that the event horizons *could* get smaller. But at the time, this was a major accomplishment.

During the 1970s, Stephen was becoming more respected in the science world, but he was still fighting for his basic rights as a disabled person. At the time, Britain was not very aware of the needs of disabled and chronically ill people. Jane became a vocal public advocate for disabled peoples' rights. She and Stephen asked Cambridge University to improve its buildings' accessibility for the disabled. They also spoke to the City of Cambridge about creating a wheelchair ramp at the Arts Theatre and at the cinema. Eventually, their requests were granted. Then they went even further and asked for improvements at the English National Opera in London and the Royal Opera House at Covent Garden.

In 1971, Stephen published an essay titled "Black Holes" that won the Gravity Research Foundation Award. Two years later, in 1973, he published his first book, *The Large-Scale Structure of Space-Time*. He wrote it with his longtime colleague and good friend, George Ellis. The book talked about the big-picture properties of the universe.

But around this time, Stephen began to focus more on the study of quantum gravity and quantum mechanics, which was a different branch of physics. Quantum mechanics tried to understand the universe on a small scale; it was the physics of molecules and particles. Up until this time, Stephen had always dealt with the big picture, using mathematics and ideas of general relativity to come up with theories about how the large bodies, such as black holes and stars, of the universe worked. However, the laws of general relativity (which deals with very large objects) and the laws of thermodynamics and quantum mechanics (which deals with very small objects on the molecular level) contradicted each other. These laws applied to the universe in their own context, but they couldn't apply together at the same time.

Now, the scientific world was beginning to wonder if the big-picture laws of general relativity (which Stephen worked with) and the small-scale laws of quantum mechanics could be connected. Scientists wondered if there were some general law of the universe that could unify all these different laws and branches of physics. It was every physicist's dream to answer this question.

In search of answers, Stephen went to conferences in Poland and Russia with Jane in 1973, leaving their children behind with their grandparents. Following his research and discussions with scientists in Moscow, Stephen was fascinated by the idea that black holes actually emitted information, instead of being complete vacuums. Two Russian physicists, Yakov Borisovich Zel'dovich and Alexei Starobinsky, had suggested that according to the "uncertainty principle" of quantum mechanics, black holes should emit particles.

This was an interesting thought, and it was a way of applying quantum mechanics to massive bodies in the universe. But there was no way to prove it—at least not yet. Stephen rose to the challenge and tried to figure out a solution mathematically. A year later, he was ready to reveal his findings. They would come to rock the world.

On February 14, 1974, Stephen announced his new theory about black holes at a lecture in Oxford. Contrary to all previous thought, his calculations revealed that black holes do indeed emit energy. He also came to the conclusion that this energy, or radiation, flies through space until it eventually evaporates. With this one theory, Stephen Hawking changed the scientific world's idea that black holes were places where no information could escape. Black holes were not, in fact, complete vacuums. This became the theory that we now call Hawking radiation.

This was a breakthrough that came one step closer not only to understanding how black holes work, but also to unifying quantum physics and thermodynamics (the laws of the small) to general relativity (the laws of the large). Scientists saw it as an important step towards finding the "theory of everything" that would finally unify the branches of physics. This theory launched Stephen to the highest levels of the science world.

Just a month later, Stephen Hawking was elected to become a Fellow of the Royal Society. This was an honor that most scientists received at the end of their careers, after they had achieved a lifetime of work. Stephen was only thirty-two years old, and he still had many more accomplishments ahead of him.

That same year, Stephen was offered a visiting fellowship for the year at the California Technical Institute of Technology in Pasadena. Stephen and his family accepted the invitation, but they knew that they would need extra help. By this time Stephen was no longer able to feed, bathe, or dress himself. They decided to bring two of his students, Bernard Carr and Peter De'Ath, to help Stephen with his lectures and his daily needs.

Stephen earned more awards and medals in the years that followed: in 1975, he was awarded the Eddington Medal from the Royal Astronomical Society and the Pope Pius XI Gold Medal for science. In 1976, he won the Dannie Heineman Prize, the Hughes Medal, and the Maxwell Prize.

Then, in 1977, Stephen was given a permanent position at Cambridge University. It was a major relief for the family, who did not know what would happen once Stephen's special fellowship at Cambridge expired. Instead, he became a "reader," or associate professor, at the university. He became very busy with appearances, lectures, and conferences around the world. With his discovery of Hawking radiation, he had become a science celebrity who was very much in demand.

More good fortune soon followed. In 1977,

Cambridge University gave Stephen a promotion: he became a professor of gravitational physics. Then, in 1978, he received an honorary doctorate from the University of Oxford as well as the Albert Einstein Medal.

Despite all these achievements, however, his physical state was always getting worse. His home life was becoming more and more difficult as Jane struggled to care for Stephen in addition to their two growing children. Robert, who was now about nine years old, was beginning to take up some of the responsibilities of caring for his father. He helped dress and feed him, and sometimes even took him to the bathroom.

Meanwhile, Stephen became a point of British national pride. The media couldn't get enough of Stephen Hawking. In articles and on television programs, he was portrayed as a genius as well as a brave man overcoming disability. A short biography of his life was featured in a two-hour BBC presentation about physics. The program, called "The Key to the Universe," aired all over the world. Stephen's own words ended the show:

The Big Bang is like a black hole but on a much larger scale. By finding out how a black hole creates matter we may understand how the Big Bang created all the matter in the Universe. The singularity in the Big Bang seems to be a frontier beyond which we cannot go. Yet we can't help asking what lies beyond the Big Bang. Why does the Universe exist at all?
My son Robert is always asking questions. Why this? Why that? Every child does. It is what raises us from being cavemen.
On one view, we are just weak, feeble creatures at the mercy of the forces of Nature. When we discover the laws that govern those forces we rise above them and become masters of the Universe.

With these words, Stephen Hawking revealed something very true and intimate about his own life: although he could not be a master of his own body, his ability to understand the laws of nature made him a master of the universe.

International Fame and a Brush with Death

Stephen was working in an exciting time for astrophysics. During the 1970s and 1980s, the general public was becoming more aware and interested in black holes and questions about the origin of the universe. As Stephen continued his work in general relativity and quantum mechanics, astrophysics became more mainstream and popular in the media. Television programs on the universe, such as Carl Sagan's *Cosmos*, no doubt made these topics more accessible to the general public. Amidst this excitement, Stephen Hawking stood at the very front of black hole research. In just a few years, Stephen would reach the height of his international fame with the 1988 publication of his book, *A Brief History of Time*.

Before he wrote the book, however, several significant events occurred in the late 1970s and early 1980s. In 1979, his third child, Timothy, was born. By this time, Stephen was thirty-seven years old. Motor neuron disease had taken away his ability to walk, talk, and do most things for himself. The most movement he had was to control the hand-held stick attached to his motorized wheelchair. In a sense, the muscles in his body could not degenerate much more. This was somewhat of a relief, as he was still just as mentally active and strong as ever. The biggest threat to his health was not motor neuron disease itself, but rather, the common cold.

All of Stephen's daily care and most of his medical care still came from his wife, Jane. However, with the birth of Timothy, she was finding it harder and harder to be a full-time nurse to Stephen, as well as a mother to their three children. This is why, by 1979, the Hawking household had a frequent visitor by the name of Jonathan Hellyer Jones. He and Jane had become friends in 1977, when Jane began singing in his choir as a much-needed break from her daily chores. Jonathan began to help Jane with her responsibilities, and also to help care for Stephen and the children. Although Jonathan and Jane developed romantic feelings for each other, they kept their relationship platonic for a long time. Stephen accepted this arrangement, seeing that it helped Jane and kept the family stable.

Just a few months after the birth of his third child, Stephen Hawking was given yet another honor. He was appointed the Lucasian Professor in Mathematics at Cambridge University. This is the highest academic position at Cambridge. In fact, it is perhaps one of the highest academic honors in the world. Sir Isaac Newton held the chair from 1669 to

1702. The appointment cemented Stephen's prestige as a scientist, mathematician, and great thinker in the academic world. He made an acceptance speech that was translated to the audience by one of his students.

However, around Christmas of 1979, disaster struck. Just a few months after his appointment to the chair, the entire Hawking household came down with a bad cold. Although Jane and the children were able to recover on their own, motor neuron disease made Stephen's recovery very difficult. The muscles in his throat were so weak that it was difficult for him to breathe. He choked and coughed day and night. Because Jane still had to take care of a newborn baby, it was decided that Stephen should go into a nursing home to have nurses and doctors help him get over his cold.

While Stephen recovered at the nursing home, Martin Rees, the Plumian Professor of Astronomy and Experimental Philosophy at Cambridge (who today is the Astronomer

Royal), met with Jane and urged her to hire home nurses for Stephen. Previously, this had never been an option because at-home medical care was so expensive. Also, Stephen had refused all this time to hire medical staff. Instead, Stephen had always hired graduate students to help him at home, at his office, and during his travels. The students took some pressure off of Jane and the family, but it was not enough. Those who were close to Stephen could see that he needed professional medical care. Martin Rees offered to find the funding for at-home medical care for Stephen if Jane could find a suitable nurse.

Jane was able to find a group of nurses who could help the family care for Stephen. When Stephen came home from the nursing home mostly recovered, he initially resisted the new at-home nurses. However, he eventually accepted the routine. Soon, he found that he did not have to depend completely on his family and students to care for him. It was, in a sense, freeing for everyone.

International Fame and a Brush with Death

Despite Stephen's delicate condition, the awards, honors, medals, and titles kept coming from all over the world, and he continued to travel. In 1981 Stephen was invited to the Vatican in Rome and named a lifetime member of the Pontifical Academy. In 1982, Stephen was named a Commander of the British Empire, an honorary award given by the Queen of England. His oldest son, Robert, escorted him to receive the medal from the queen.

During all this time, Stephen kept his political and philosophical principles strong. He was not just active in his field of cosmology, but he was also a vocal activist for social issues as well. In his youth he had been a devoted socialist who was never afraid to voice his opinions. He was even known to argue with his elders and others who perhaps should have been treated with more respect.

Stephen rose to fame during the height of the Cold War tensions. As students, Stephen and Jane had been active members of the

Campaign for Nuclear Disarmament. They continued to uphold this political stance. When Stephen was awarded the Franklin Medal in 1981, he used his acceptance speech as a platform to speak out about nuclear disarmament. At the Franklin Institute in Philadelphia, he addressed a crowd of Americans. Using his vast knowledge of the universe, he explained the dangers of nuclear power. It took four billion years for mammals to evolve, he said. It took about four million years for humans to evolve, and it took about four hundred years for humans to develop modern-day technology. In the last forty years, he continued, humans had come very close to understanding the connections among the different branches of physics. Once they figured this out and discovered a unified theory, humans would be able to explain anything and everything in the universe. However, he said, all this progress could be destroyed in just forty minutes with one nuclear disaster. He told the crowd that this was the biggest problem facing current society.

Stephen was also recognized around the world as an activist for the rights of disabled people. Since about the late 1970s, the rights of disabled people had become more of a mainstream issue. To spread awareness and publicity, Stephen became the "Patients' Patron" of the Motor Neuron Disease Association. He also became the Vice President of the Leonard Cheshire Foundation.

Stephen's untiring thoughts and theories on the universe continued. During the 1980s, Stephen was busy writing a series of essays with Werner Israel, a Canadian physicist. They were trying to reconcile relativity with quantum physics. As the Lucasian Professor, Stephen was now a renowned and valuable enough person at Cambridge that he could arrange seminars and spend a lot of university money to invite great thinkers from all over the world. He recorded and analyzed the dialogue of these seminars and published them as essays.

Next, Hawking tackled theories on the beginning of the universe. In 1983, Stephen Hawking and fellow physicist Jim Hartle developed an idea called the "Hartle–Hawking state." This idea said that if you were to travel back in time to the very beginning of the universe, you would find space, but not time. And because there was no time before the Big Bang, the "beginning" of the universe does not exist. This meant that the universe has no origin at all—at least not in the sense that we understand an "origin" as a point in time. This was a revolutionary idea and is still considered a valid theory by many astrophysicists today.

Stephen seemed to be on an unstoppable path to fame and fortune during the 1980s. However, the laws of physics apply even to human daily life. In this case, entropy—or the law that states everything had potential for destruction and disorder—was about to become tested and proven for Stephen and his family.

International Fame and a Brush with Death

Early 1985 had been a pleasant time—Stephen had finished his first draft of *A Brief History of Time*, the book that would make him world-famous. The draft was being reviewed by Bantam Books, a large publisher in New York. Then, in the summer of 1985, Stephen and his family traveled to Geneva. He was on a mission to talk with particle physicists who worked at CERN (the European Organization for Nuclear Research). While his family toured the Lake Geneva area, Stephen went on to Geneva for his scientific talks. However, as he traveled, he developed a bad cough that worried his nurses and students. Although Stephen tried to assure them that he was fine, they called a doctor. The doctor diagnosed him with pneumonia and sent him to the hospital. To everyone's shock, his illness appeared life threatening.

Stephen was put on a heavy dose of medication and life support to help him breathe. In the intensive care unit, he remained in a drugged, unconscious state until Jane and the family cut their holiday short and rushed to the hospital.

The doctors explained that Stephen had been put on heavy medication to allow a tube to be inserted into his throat to help him breathe. However, if Stephen was taken off of the drugs, he was so ill that there was a chance he would not survive. The doctor gave Jane the choice of taking him off of life support, and thus ending his life, or giving Stephen a tracheotomy. A tracheotomy surgery would insert a tube permanently into his throat, allowing him to breathe without his throat muscles. However, the operation would take away his ability to speak completely.

Jane refused to simply let Stephen die. However, she did not want to assume that he would need a tracheotomy either. Instead, they took him off of life support and closely watched his condition to see if he would recover on his own. However, weeks later it became clear that he needed the tracheotomy. He had the operation, and, over many months,

INTERNATIONAL FAME AND A BRUSH WITH DEATH

returned to his normal health.

But now Stephen's life had a new complication: The tracheotomy tube needed regular cleaning and monitoring. It was a specialized medical device that was also a potential source of infection. It required 24-hour medical care by people who were trained in how to change, clean, and care for tracheotomy tubes. This would be another major expense for the household—an expense that the Hawkings couldn't afford.

One of Stephen's colleagues suggested writing to the MacArthur Foundation in America for a medical grant. Although the grant expired and had to be renewed every year, at least it would cover the costs of medical care for the short term. Jane wrote to the board of directors and was awarded a yearlong grant. But this was only half the battle. Now suitable nurses had to be found and hired. After long hours and many interviews, Jane and Stephen's personal assistant were able to arrange a rotation of nurses to provide 24-hour medical care for Stephen in eight-hour shifts. In total, medical bills for Stephen's care came to £36,000 per year. And another change was introduced into the Hawking household: one of the nurses hired was named Elaine Mason. She would come to play a bigger role in Stephen's life.

After Stephen lost his ability to speak, he continued to communicate with the help of a computer provided by Intel Corporation. It allowed him to choose words with a hand-held control to create sentences. This device was modified and attached to his wheelchair so he could communicate at any time, in any place. The device was freeing for Stephen, because he could now communicate with anyone, whereas before, he had needed a family member or student to interpret his slurred, quiet speech. Now he could get his point across without anybody's help or interpretation. However, this new device also didn't come without certain costs. Attaching it to his wheelchair made Stephen even harder to lift over curbs, up stairs, etc. The chair itself was already very heavy with its motor, batteries, and various parts. With Stephen in the chair, it all weighed roughly 300 pounds.

By December 1985, after spending months in the hospital, Stephen had regained much of his health. He was now well enough to make short visits to his office at Cambridge. He was also well enough to begin editing his book, *A Brief History in Time*. In fact, one of his first requests voiced on his new computer communication device was for his assistant to help him edit his book.

Writing *A Brief History of Time*

In 1982, Stephen had decided it was time to write a book about physics for the general public. Part of the decision was financial—although Stephen enjoyed worldwide fame, medals and awards could not support his family.

With the help of his students, he had written a draft of *A Brief History of Time*, a book about cosmology and the origins of the universe. It discussed a wide range of topics, including early theories of how the universe worked as well as modern-day theories. To the non-scientific reader, it explained many complex concepts in physics, mathematics, and cosmology, such as the Big Bang, light cones, black holes, and particle physics. It was an inspiring work with a dramatic conclusion. In closing, Stephen wrote that he "looked forward to a time when mankind would be able to 'know the mind of God' through the formulation...of a compete unified theory of the universe, the theory of everything."

Although Stephen had finished his draft in 1984, it took months for his agent to find a publisher who was interested. He was finally approached by the American publisher Bantam Books, who gave Stephen a contract and $250,000 to publish his book. Nobody knew at the time that it would become an instant bestseller and popularize the study of the universe like no other book had ever done.

In 1985, everything was set to go to begin work on preparing the book for publication, but Stephen fell ill in Geneva. After Stephen's return to the department that December, he finally began to address the edits the New York publisher had given.

Stephen soon saw that there was much work to be done. The editor had said that the book was too dense and complicated, and not publishable for a general audience. He also said that every equation included in the book would cut sales by half. He insisted on taking all the equations out. With some frustration, Stephen realized the book would have to be rewritten.

But, with the help of his new speech computer, Stephen was able to write his second draft more easily than before. By 1987, Stephen had finished the rewrite. He took some time searching for the perfect title. Then, in 1988, it was published, first to an American audience, then to a British one. Its full title was *A Brief History of Time: From the Big Bang to Black Holes*. He dedicated it to his wife, Jane.

Stephen's family eagerly waited to see how the public would respond to the book.

Although the Hawkings didn't expect the book to be a bestseller, they hoped that it would bring in another income stream. As a household that supported the needs of three growing children as well as Stephen's medical bills, they could use all the financial help they could get.

What nobody expected was that it would become an immediate bestseller. The book went on to sell more than 10 million copies in twenty years. To date, it has been translated into thirty-five languages. Stephen once said, "I knew it was going to be a success when it was translated into Serbo-Croatian." It remained on the *London Sunday Times* bestseller list for more than four years. Today, it is certainly the most well-known and well-read book on astrophysics written for a non-scientific audience.

A Sad Period

After the publication of *A Brief History of Time* people would call at all hours of the day asking to speak to Stephen Hawking. Some people even showed up at the house. Suddenly, Stephen was invited to travel from country to country, promoting his book. On these international book tours, Stephen would instantly be recognized on the street, and people would stand and applaud as he passed by. More and more media attention followed. Although this was a major triumph for Stephen, it caused some trouble in his home life. His incredible

A Sad Period

fame and fast-growing wealth seemed to distance him from his wife and children, especially as he became more dependent on his nurses rather than his family.

When Stephen traveled, his team of nurses always accompanied him. Even when he was at home, a nurse would always be there to fulfill his every need and wish. Although the 24-hour medical help was a big relief for the family, the introduction of outsiders into the house threw off the Hawkings' delicate family dynamic.

In the Hawking household, the family's various relationships were something that everyone had worked for many years to create and preserve. The relationship between Stephen and Jane was very special and, of course, very challenging. The relationship between Jane and Jonathan also required much self-control and sacrifice from both parties. The relationship between Jonathan and Stephen was also delicate, as well as each of the children's relations with each other and with the adults. It was a careful balancing act that required patience and understanding from every person involved.

But once the nurses arrived in the household, the delicate balance was broken. There were arguments over how things should be done in the home, whose needs took priority, and how best to care for Stephen. Jane often felt like she was coming under attack by the nurses. The children often felt that their needs were not as important as Stephen's. Jonathan became the victim of the nurses' bad-mouthing. But the biggest problem, according to many of Stephen's family and friends, was one of his nurses, Elaine Mason.

A handsome and vibrant nurse, Elaine was a striking figure. She had long, red, curly hair and a pretty smile. She was a married mother of two, as well as a strong and capable nurse. She could lift Stephen out of his chair all by herself. But she also had a very strong personality and was extremely protective of Stephen. This often created conflict in the household

A Sad Period

among the nurses and the Hawkings.

Elaine was devoted to Stephen, and interestingly, so was her husband, David. A software engineer, David was the one who helped adapt Stephen's speech computer when he lost his voice in 1985. However, the friendly feelings and the support network that surrounded Stephen were all about to change.

During the late 1980s, Stephen became more and more dependent on Elaine. Jane found herself being replaced as Stephen's head carer and confidant. Finally, one day in 1989, the truth came out: Stephen had fallen in love with Elaine and he was going to leave Jane.

According to *Traveling to Infinity: My Life with Stephen*, a memoir written by Jane, Stephen wrote her a letter to announce that he was leaving. He moved out of their home on 5 West Road, Cambridge, in 1990. However, his children were still very important to him and he insisted on seeing Tim, his youngest child, at least twice a week.

Stephen and Jane finalized their divorce

in 1995. He married Elaine Mason several months later, in September of 1995. He seemed very happy and is known to have said, "It's wonderful—I've married the woman I love." However, looking back on the difficult times, Stephen's daughter Lucy has commented that she was often frustrated by the nurses who disrupted the Hawking household, as well as by Stephen's rapid rise to celebrity. "The minute he got fame and money he was gone," she said.

Then came a period in Stephen's life that

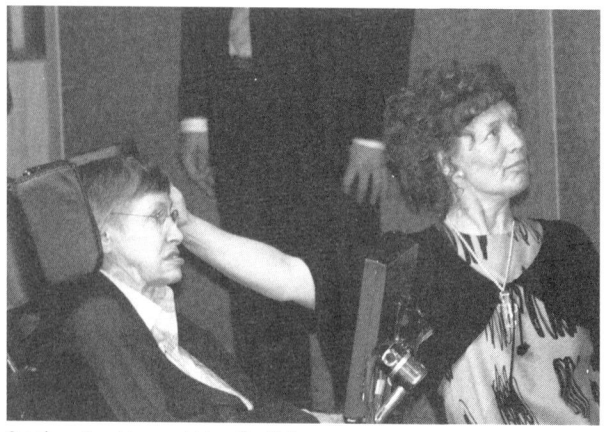

Stephen Hawking and his wife, Elain.

A Sad Period

frightened and saddened his loved ones. For some years after Stephen's marriage to Elaine, Stephen's nurses, colleagues, and family members began to suspect something chilling: they thought Elaine was emotionally and physically abusing Stephen. Sometime after his second marriage, he began to have mysterious injuries—bruises on his body, swollen limbs, a broken wrist, a black eye, a cut lip, and more. In 1999, fearing the worst, Stephen's daughter Lucy went to Neil McKendrick, the Master of Gonville and Caius College. She told him that she feared her father was being abused. The police looked into the matter but Stephen denied the charges. Without accusations from Stephen, the police were not able to build a case.

However, Stephen's other nurses and assistants began to speak out and say they had witnessed Elaine's violent temper. They said Elaine verbally abused Stephen, screaming at him and using terrible language. Some nurses had actually seen her physically harm him. One of Stephen's former assistants, Sue Masey, said she had to quit her job because she couldn't stand to see what was happening to Stephen. According to a 2004 *Vanity Fair* article, she said, "I left Stephen because I couldn't stand it. Elaine is a monster."

However, none of the Hawking family had ever witnessed any abuse, and the nurses were legally required to keep patient matters private. For a period of about five years, Stephen's family and friends continued to make complaints to the police about abuse, but Stephen continued to deny all charges. He once even told Lucy to stop interfering in his life. And so, the case against Elaine was dropped each time. Meanwhile, Stephen's relations with his ex-wife Jane and his children were mostly cut off.

This unhappy time in Stephen's life ended in 2006, when Stephen and Elaine divorced. Stephen began to reach out to Jane and his three children again. Today, Jane (who is now married to Jonathan Hellyer Jones) and the three children are on friendly terms with Stephen again. Jane and Jonathan live quite close to Stephen in Cambridge. They often meet for lunch and celebrate birthdays and other events together.

Into the 21st Century

At the turn of the century, Hawking remains a relevant and leading scientist. He published another popular science book, *The Universe in a Nutshell*, in 2001. It was, in a sense, a follow-up book to *A Brief History of Time*. It explained complex concepts in theoretical physics and won the Aventis Prize for Science Books in 2002. That same year, the BBC conducted a nation-wide vote on the 100 Greatest Britons. Citizens of the UK voted for Stephen Hawking to be included on that list.

Even today, Stephen continues to strive

to make physics accessible to the public. In 2005, he published *A Briefer History of Time*, a work that further simplifies his original *A Brief History of Time*. It also updates many of Stephen's initial theories and thoughts, as scientific progress over the years has changed or fine-tuned many of these concepts.

It is interesting to note, too, that some scientific breakthroughs have disproved some of Stephen's theories. One example is Stephen's idea of the loss of information in a black hole, known as the second law of black holes. Throughout the years, many physicists, scientists, and mathematicians challenged this theory. Although Stephen tried to defend his theory, he recently admitted defeat. In 2014, Stephen called his idea "his biggest blunder."

Still, despite a disproven theory or two, Stephen Hawking continues to win awards, honors, and medals from all around the world. In 2006, he won the Copley Medal from the Royal Society, which is the oldest scientific medal awarded by the prestigious group. Some say it is the oldest scientific medal in the world. In 2009, he won the Presidential Medal of Freedom, which is America's highest honor awarded to civilians. Just recently, in 2013, Stephen won Russia's Special Fundamental Physics Prize. To date, he has not won a Nobel Prize, although he was rumored to have been a candidate in the 1970s.

In many ways, Stephen Hawking is still a darling of mainstream media. He has broken through popular barriers like no other scientist or physicist has. One of his most memorable appearances in the media happened in 2007, when he participated in a zero-gravity flight sponsored by Zero Gravity Corporation. For Stephen, it was a way to raise public awareness about the amazing things that disabled people can accomplish if given a chance. It was also a way to increase public interest in space. On that flight, he became weightless eight times, and the whole world delighted in photos and videos of him floating in midair.

"It was wonderful," Stephen said after the flight. "I could have gone on and on. Space, here I come!"

Stephen Hawking has also successfully reached out to younger audiences. After Stephen reconnected with his family, he co-wrote a children's book about space with his daughter Lucy. *George's Secret Key to the Universe*, which came out in 2007, is a picture book that explains theoretical physics and the universe to children. Later, Lucy and Stephen published follow-up books, *George's Cosmic*

Treasure Hunt and *George and the Big Bang*, in 2009 and 2011, respectively. Some have said the characters in these books are similar to members of the Hawking family. Stephen has also bridged the popular culture gap in appearances in shows like *The Simpsons*.

However, as time passes, Stephen continues to battle with motor neuron disease. In 2005, he lost the use of his hand. Today, Stephen controls his speech computer by a muscle in his cheek. His cheek movements are detected by an infrared sensor on his eyeglasses, which sends the information to the computer. In this way, Stephen can create about one word a minute. Surprisingly, the digital voice that reads Stephen's sentences out loud is said to have an American accent. Although there are other voice technologies available, Stephen has chosen to remain with his original voice. He says he identifies with it.

Currently, Intel is working on a communication device that reads facial expressions, and Stephen has also experimented with brain-controlled interfaces to help him speak. These new technologies have yet to be perfected but are very exciting.

Stephen retired from his post as the Lucasian Professor of Mathematics in 2009. Today, at seventy-four years old, he has outlived his original doctors' prognosis by an amazing fifty-one years. He is still active in his role as one of the world's most brilliant physicists and as an ambassador of science to the general public. His lectures continue to pack famous halls and academic institutions, such as the University of Berkeley, the California Institute of Technology, and the Ferni National Accelerator Laboratory. Stephen sums up his continuing popularity and celebrity status with a very self-aware comment: "No one can resist the idea of a crippled genius."

Stephen Hawking has contributed an incredible amount of knowledge to humankind, not just in the science world, but also in the world of disability rights and understanding.

The story of his life and his ability to overcome difficult challenges to meet his full potential is truly inspiring.

Word List

- 本文で使われている全ての語を掲載しています（LEVEL 1, 2）。ただし、LEVEL 3 以上は、中学校レベルの語を含みません。
- 語形が規則変化する語の見出しは原形で示しています。不規則変化語は本文中で使われている形になっています。
- 一般的な意味を紹介していますので、一部の語で本文で実際に使われている品詞や意味と合っていないことがあります。
- 品詞は以下のように示しています。

名 名詞	代 代名詞	形 形容詞	副 副詞	動 動詞	助 助動詞
前 前置詞	接 接続詞	間 間投詞	冠 冠詞	略 略語	俗 俗語
頭 接頭語	尾 接尾語	号 記号	関 関係代名詞		

A

- **a ~ or two** 2, 3の
- **ability** 名（〜する）能力
- **about to** 《be -》まさに〜しようとしている、〜するところだ
- **absolutely** 副完全に、全面的に
- **abuse** 動虐待する 名虐待
  verbally abuse 口汚くののしる
- **academic** 形①学校の、大学の ②学問の
- **accelerator** 名加速器
- **accent** 名アクセント、口調
- **accept** 動①受け入れる ②同意する、認める
- **acceptance speech** 受賞スピーチ、就任演説
- **accessibility** 名行きやすいこと、アクセスしやすさ
- **accessible** 形身近な、とっつきやすい
- **accompany** 動ついていく、つきそう
- **accomplish** 動成し遂げる、果たす
- **accomplishment** 名業績
- **according to** 〜によれば［よると］
- **accusation** 名告訴、告発
- **achieve** 動成し遂げる、達成する、成功を収める
- **achievement** 名業績
- **act** 名行為、行い
- **active** 形活動的な
- **activist** 名活動家
- **actually** 副実際に、本当に
- **Adams Prize** アダムス賞《ケンブリッジ大学が主催する数学科学分野の功績を称える賞》
- **adapt** 動〜を適応させる
- **addition** 名追加《in -》加えて
- **address** 動①対処する、取り組む ②演説をする、話しかける
- **admiration** 名賞賛、感嘆
- **admit** 動認める
- **adopt** 動養子にする
- **adult** 名大人
- **advisor** 名助言者、顧問
- **advocate** 名提唱者、支持者
- **afford** 動《can -》〜する（経済的・時間的な）余裕がある
- **afterward** 副その後、のちに

76

Word List

- **age** 熟 at the age of ～歳のときに
- **agent** 名 代理人
- **ahead of** ～より先[前]に, ～に先んじて
- **air raid** 空襲, 空爆
- **Albert Einstein Medal** アルベルト・アインシュタイン・メダル《アインシュタイン協会主催のアインシュタインに関連する科学研究や業績を称える賞》
- **Alexei Starobinsky** アレクセイ・スタロビンスキー《人名。ロシアの天体物理学者。1948–》
- **all by oneself** 自分だけで, 独力で
- **allow** 動《– … to ～》…が～するのを可能にする
- **ALS** 略 筋萎縮性側索硬化症(= amyotrophic lateral sclerosis)
- **although** 接 ～だけれども, ～にもかかわらず, たとえ～でも
- **always** 熟 not always 必ずしも～であるとは限らない
- **amazing** 形 驚くべき
- **ambassador** 名 使者, 大使
- **America** 名 アメリカ《国名・大陸》
- **American** 形 アメリカ(人)の 名 アメリカ人
- **amidst** 前 ～のまん中に[で]
- **amount** 名 量, 価値
- **amyotrophic** 形 筋萎縮性の
  amyotrophic lateral sclerosis 筋萎縮性側索硬化症
- **analyze** 動 分析する, 細かく検討する
- **and so** それだから, それで
- **anniversary** 名 記念日
- **announce** 動 (人に)知らせる, 公表する
- **annual** 形 年1回の
- **another** 熟 yet another さらにもう一つの

- **any time** いつでも
- **anybody** 代《疑問文・条件節で》誰か
- **anymore** 副《通例否定文, 疑問文で》今はもう
- **anyone** 代《肯定文で》誰でも
- **apartment** 名 アパート
- **appear** 動 (～のように)見える, ～らしい
- **appearance** 名 登場, 出演
- **applaud** 動 拍手かっさいする, 賞賛する
- **application** 名 申し込み
- **apply** 動 ①申し込む, 志願する ②あてはまる, 適合する
- **appoint** 動 任命する
- **appointment** 名 任命
- **approach** 動 話を持ちかける
- **argue** 動 ①論じる, 議論する ②主張する
- **argument** 名 議論, 論争
- **arrange** 動 取り決める, 手はずを整える
- **arrangement** 名 取り決め
- **arrive in** ～に着く
- **article** 名 (新聞・雑誌などの)記事, 論文
- **as** 熟 as ever 相変わらず, これまでのように as if あたかも～のように, まるで～みたいに as much as ～と同じだけ as well as ～と同様に, ～だけでなく…も as ～ as ever 相変わらず ～ as ～ as one can できる限り～
- **ask ～ if** ～に…かどうか尋ねる
- **assign** 動 割り当てる
- **assistant** 名 助手, 補佐
- **associate professor** 准教授
- **association** 名 協会, 組合
- **assume** 動 見なす, 当然のことと思う

- □ **assure** 動 ～を確信させる
- □ **astronomer** 名 天文学者 Astronomer Royal 王室天文官, グリニッジ天文台長
- □ **astronomical** 形 天文学の
- □ **astronomy** 名 天文学
- □ **astrophysicist** 名 天体[宇宙]物理学者
- □ **astrophysics** 名 天体物理学
- □ **at** 熟 at all そもそも, 一体 at first 最初は, 初めのうちは at least 少なくとも at the age of ～歳のときに at the end of ～の終わりに at the time そのころ, 当時は
- □ **at-home** 形 在宅の, 家庭用の
- □ **atom** 名 原子
- □ **attach** 動 取り付ける
- □ **attack** 動 非難する come under attack 非難の的になる
- □ **attend** 動 ①出席する, 参加する ②(学校などに)通う
- □ **attention** 名 注目
- □ **audience** 名 聴衆, 読者
- □ **autobiography** 名 自伝, 自叙伝
- □ **available** 形 利用[使用・入手]できる
- □ **Aventis Prize for Science Books** アベンティス科学図書賞《大手製薬会社アベンティス社が主催した賞》
- □ **award** 動 (賞などを)与える, 授与する 名 賞
- □ **aware** 形 ①気がついて, 知って ②(～の)認識のある be aware of ～に気がついている
- □ **awareness** 名 認識
- □ **awful** 形 ひどい, 恐ろしい

B

- □ **bad-mouthing** 形 口の悪い
- □ **balance** 名 均衡, 落ち着き 動 釣り合いをとる
- □ **ball** 名 (大)舞踏会 May Ball メイボール《ケンブリッジ大学で年度末に行われる学生主催の舞踏会》
- □ **bang** 名 衝撃音, バン[ドスン・バタン]という音 Big Bang ビッグバン《宇宙の初めに発生し現在の膨張宇宙に至ったとされる大爆発》
- □ **Bantam Books** バンタム・ブックス《社名, アメリカの出版社》
- □ **barrier** 名 垣根, 境界
- □ **based on** (be ～)～に基づく
- □ **basic** 形 基本的
- □ **Basil King** バジル・キング《人名, ホーキング博士の学生時代の友人》
- □ **basis** 名 基礎, 原理, 根拠
- □ **bathe** 動 風呂に入る
- □ **bathroom** 名 手洗い, トイレ
- □ **Battelle Memorial Institute** バテル記念研究所《米国に本社を置く非営利の科学技術企業》
- □ **battery** 名 電池, バッテリー
- □ **battle** 名 戦い
- □ **BBC** 名 英国放送協会
- □ **because of** ～のために, ～の理由で
- □ **bee** 名 ミツバチ
- □ **beginning** 名 初め, 始まり
- □ **belief** 名 信念
- □ **believe in** ～を信じる
- □ **Berkeley** 名 バークレー《地名》
- □ **Bernard Carr** バーナード・カー《人名, ホーキング博士が教えている学生》
- □ **bestseller** 名 売れ行きがいい本, ベストセラー
- □ **between A and B** AとBの間に
- □ **beyond** 前 ～を越えて, ～の向こうに
- □ **Big Bang** ビッグバン《宇宙の初め

に発生し現在の膨張宇宙に至ったとされる大爆発》
- **big-picture** 形 大局の見地から見た
- **bill** 名 請求書
- **billion** 名 10億
- **biography** 名 伝記, 一代記
- **birth** 名 出産, 誕生 give birth 出産する
- **black hole** ブラックホール black hole dynamics ブラックホール力学
- **blame on** ～のせいにする
- **blunder** 名 大失敗, へま
- **board game** ボードゲーム
- **board of directors** 重役会, 役員会
- **body** 名 (1)肉体, 身体 (2)物体, 天体
- **bonding** 名 絆, 同士愛
- **boring** 形 うんざりさせる, 退屈な
- **both A and B** AもBも
- **bowtie** 名 蝶ネクタイ
- **brain-controlled** 形 脳波で制御する
- **branch** 名 分野, 部門
- **brave** 形 勇敢な
- **break through** ～を打ち破る
- **breakthrough** 名 飛躍的な前進, (行き詰まりなどの)突破, 解明
- **breathe** 動 呼吸する
- **brick** 形 レンガ造りの
- **brief** 形 (1)短い時間の (2)簡単な A Brief History of Time『ホーキング, 宇宙を語る』《邦題》
- **brilliant** 形 優秀な, すばらしい
- **Britain** 名 英国, イギリス
- **Briton** 名 英国人
- **bruise** 名 打撲傷
- **brush with death** 死にひんする
- **build a case** 立件する
- **building** 名 建物, ビルディング
- **by** 熟 all by oneself 自分だけで, 独力で by oneself 一人で, 自分だけで by the time of ～の時までに by this time この時までに, もうすでに

C

- **calculation** 名 計算, 演算
- **California** 名 カリフォルニア《米国の州》
- **California Institute of Technology** カリフォルニア工科大学《米国に本部を置く私立工科大学》
- **call at** (家を)訪れる
- **Cambridge** 名 ケンブリッジ《地名》
- **Cambridge University** ケンブリッジ大学《英国の総合大学》
- **Campaign for Nuclear Disarmament** 核兵器撤廃運動《英国の反核運動団体》
- **can** 熟 as ～ as one can できる限り～
- **Canadian** 形 カナダ(人)の
- **candidate** 名 候補者
- **cannot ~ enough** いくら～してもしたりない
- **cannot help** ～せずにはいられない
- **capable** 形 有能な
- **caravan** 名 幌馬車, 移動住宅
- **care** 熟 care for ～の世話をする, ～を介護する, ～の手入れをする intensive care unit 集中治療室 take care of ～の世話をする, ～面倒を見る
- **career** 名 (生涯の・専門的な)職業, 経歴
- **carer** 名 介護者, 世話をする人
- **Carl Sagan** カール・セーガン

THE BIOGRAPHY OF STEPHEN HAWKING

《人名》米国の天文学者, SF作家, 1934-1996》
- **case** 熟 build a case 立件する
- **cast** 動 投げかける, 投じる cast a shadow on ~の上に暗い影を落とす
- **caveman** 名 洞窟に住む原始人
- **celebrate** 動 祝う, 祝福する
- **celebrity** 名 ①有名人 ②名声
- **cement** 動 強固なものにする, 補強する
- **CERN** 略 欧州原子核研究機構, セルン (= Conseil Européen pour la Recherche Nucléaire)
- **certain** 形 ある, 一定の
- **certainly** 副 確実に
- **challenge** 名 挑戦 動 挑む, 試す
- **challenging** 形 能力が試される, 難易度の高い
- **chapel** 名 礼拝堂
- **character** 名 (小説・劇などの) 登場人物
- **charge** 名 非難, 告発
- **cheek** 名 ほお
- **childbirth** 名 出産, 分娩
- **childhood** 名 幼年 [子ども] 時代
- **chilling** 形 身も凍るような
- **choice** 名 選択 (の範囲・自由)
- **choir** 名 聖歌隊
- **choke** 動 息が詰まる, 窒息する
- **chore** 名 雑用, 雑役
- **Christmas** 名 クリスマス
- **chronically** 副 慢性的に
- **cinema** 名 映画館
- **circle** 名 社会, 分野
- **citizen** 名 市民, 住民
- **civilian** 名 一般市民, 民間人
- **cleaning** 名 掃除, クリーニング
- **clear** 形 はっきりした, 明白な
- **clever** 形 頭のよい, 利口な
- **cleverness** 名 賢さ
- **climb into** ~に乗り込む
- **close to** 《be ~》~に近い
- **closely** 副 念入りに, ぴったり近くで
- **closing** 名 終わり, 結び in closing 締めくくりに
- **clubhouse** 名 部室, クラブハウス
- **clumsy** 形 ぎこちない, おぼつかない
- **coincidence** 名 (偶然の) 一致
- **cold** 名 風邪
- **Cold War** 冷戦《第二次世界大戦後の米ソ二大陣営の対立。1947-1991》
- **collaborate** 動 共同研究する
- **collaboration** 名 共同研究
- **collapse** 名 崩壊 動 崩壊する, 崩れる
- **colleague** 名 同僚, 仲間
- **come** 熟 come down with (病気などに) かかる come in 現れる come out 発表される, はっきり分かる come under attack 非難の的になる come up with ~を思いつく, 考え出す, 見つけ出す
- **comfortable** 形 十分な, 安心できるだけの
- **Commander of the British Empire** 名 大英帝国勲章
- **comment** 名 論評, コメント 動 注解する, コメントする
- **common cold** 風邪
- **commonly** 副 一般に
- **communicate** 動 理解し合う
- **communication** 名 伝えること, 連絡
- **compete** 動 立ち向かう
- **complaint** 名 苦情, 告発
- **complete** 形 完全な, まったくの
- **completely** 副 完全に, すっかり
- **complex** 形 入り組んだ, 複雑な

WORD LIST

- **complicated** 形 複雑な, むずかしい
- **complication** 名 複雑な事態
- **concept** 名 概念, 観念
- **conclusion** 名 結論
- **condition** 名 (健康)状態
- **conduct** 動 実施する
- **cone** 名 円錐状の物 light cone 光円錐《四次元空間において光の道筋を表す面》
- **conference** 名 会議, 協議会
- **confidant** 名 腹心の友
- **conflict** 名 衝突, 論争
- **connect** 動 関係づける
- **connection** 名 つながり, 関係
- **consider** 動 (〜と)みなす
- **constant** 形 絶えず続く
- **context** 名 状況, 環境
- **contract** 名 契約(書)
- **contradict** 動 矛盾する, 否定する
- **contrary to** 〜に反して
- **contribute** 動 貢献する
- **control** 動 支配する, コントロールする 名 支配(力)
- **controversial** 形 物議をかもしている, 議論の的の
- **convince** 動 確信させる
- **Copley Medal** コプリ・メダル《イギリス王立協会が主催する科学業績に対して贈られる最も歴史の古い賞》
- **copy** 名 (書籍の)一部, 冊
- **Cornell University** コーネル大学《米国の大学》
- **corporation** 名 法人, (株式)会社
- **cosmic** 形 宇宙の
- **cosmology** 名 宇宙論
- **cosmos** 名 ① (the -)宇宙 ② (C-) カール・セーガンによる宇宙ブームの先駆けとなったベストセラー

- **cost** 名 費用
- **cough** 名 せき 動 せきをする
- **countryside** 名 地方, 田舎
- **county** 名 郡, 州
- **couple** 名 夫婦, カップル 動 対になる
- **course** 熟 of course もちろん, 当然
- **coursework** 名 カリキュラムに沿った授業
- **Covent Garden** コベントガーデン《地名》
- **cover** 動 補う
- **co-write** 動 〜を共同執筆する
- **coxswain** 名 舵手, 舵取り
- **create** 動 創造する, 作る, 引き起こす
- **creature** 名 生物, 動物
- **crippled** 形 手足の不自由な
- **crowd** 名 群集, 聴衆
- **curb** 名 縁石
- **curious** 形 好奇心の強い, 知りたがる
- **curly** 形 巻き毛の
- **current** 形 現在の, 目下の
- **currently** 副 今のところ, 現在
- **curse** 名 のろい
- **cut off** 切断する, 切り離す

D

- **daily** 形 毎日の, 日常の
- **Dannie Heineman Prize** ダニー・ハイネマン賞《ハイネマン財団が主催する物理学の賞》
- **dark-haired** 形 黒髪の
- **darling** 名 時代の寵児
- **date** 熟 go on a date (人と)デートする set a date 日取りを決める to

- date 今まで
- **David Mason** デイビッド・メイソン《人名。ホーキング博士の2度目の妻、エレインの元夫》
- **day** 熟 day and night 昼も夜も each day 毎日
- **deal with** ～を扱う
- **death** 名 死 brush with death 死にひんする
- **debate** 名 討論、ディベート
- **decide to do** ～することに決める
- **decision** 名 決心、決定
- **decline** 動 衰える
- **dedicate** 動 捧げる
- **deduce** 動 推論する
- **defeat** 名 敗北
- **defend** 動 弁護する、抗弁する
- **degenerate** 動 悪化する
- **degree** 名 学位
- **delicate** 形 繊細な、壊れやすい
- **delight** 動 喜ぶ 名 喜び、愉快
- **demand** 名 需要
- **Dennis Sciama** デニス・シアマ《人名。英国の物理学者。1926-1999》
- **dense** 形 ①高密度の ②難解な
- **density** 名 濃度、密度
- **deny** 動 否定する
- **department** 名 学部、学科
- **depend on** ～を頼る
- **dependent on** ～に頼っている、依存している
- **depression** 名 憂うつ、意気消沈
- **describe** 動 (言葉で)描写する、特色を述べる
- **desire** 名 欲求、願望
- **despite** 前 ～にもかかわらず
- **destroy** 動 破壊する、絶滅させる
- **destruction** 名 破壊、崩壊
- **detect** 動 検出する
- **develop** 動 ①成長させる、発展させる ②(病気などを)わずらう
- **device** 名 装置
- **devote** 動 (～を…に)捧げる
- **devoted** 形 熱心な、専念した
- **diagnose** 動 診断する
- **diagnosis** 名 診断
- **dialogue** 名 対話、話し合い
- **Diana King** ダイアナ・キング《人名。ホーキング博士の最初の妻、ジェーンの学生時代の友人》
- **digital** 形 デジタルの
- **dimension** 名 次元
- **dinnertime** 名 夕食の時間
- **director** 名 重役 board of directors 重役会、役員会
- **disability** 名 身体障害
- **disabled** 形 ①身体障害のある ②《the –》身体障害者
- **disarmament** 名 武装解除、軍備縮小 Campaign for Nuclear Disarmament 核兵器撤廃運動《英国の反核運動団体》
- **disaster** 名 厄災
- **discourage** 動 (～するのを)阻止する、やめさせる
- **discovery** 名 発見
- **discuss** 動 議論[検討]する
- **discussion** 名 討議、討論
- **disease** 名 病気 motor neuron disease 運動ニューロン疾患 tropical disease 熱帯病
- **disorder** 名 混乱、無秩序
- **disprove** 動 ～が誤りであることを証明する
- **disrupt** 動 (組織などを)分裂させる
- **distance** 名 距離、隔たり
- **distinction** 名 優秀な成績、栄達
- **divorce** 名 離婚

Word List

- **doctoral** 形 博士(号)の
- **doctorate** 名 博士号
- **don't have to** ～する必要はない
- **dose** 名 (薬剤の)1回の服用量
- **doubt** 名 疑い no doubt きっと，たぶん
- **draft** 名 下書き，草稿
- **dramatic** 形 劇的な
- **drove** 動 drive (駆り立てる)の過去
- **drug** 名 薬 動 ～に投薬する
- **due to** ～によって，～が原因で
- **dynamic** 名 動 family dynamics 家族の動態(ふれ合いなど)
- **dynamics** 名 動力学

E

- **each day** 毎日
- **each other** お互いに
- **each time** ～するたびに
- **eagerly** 副 熱心に
- **early-onset** 形 早期発症型の
- **earn** 動 ①儲ける，稼ぐ ②(名声を)博す，獲得する
- **easily** 副 容易に，簡単に
- **economy** 名 経済
- **Eddington Medal** エディントン・メダル《イギリス王立天文学会が業績ある研究者に贈る賞》
- **edit** 動 編集する 名 編集
- **editor** 名 編集者
- **education** 名 教育，教養
- **Edward Hawking** エドワード・ホーキング《人名。ホーキング博士の義弟》
- **effort** 名 努力(の成果) put time or effort into ～に時間や手間をかける
- **Elaine Mason** エレイン・メイソン《人名。看護師。ホーキング博士の2度目の妻》
- **elder** 名 《one's ～》年長者
- **elect** 動 選ぶ
- **electrode** 名 電極
- **embarrass** 動 恥ずかしい思いをさせる，困らせる
- **emit** 動 (光などを)放つ，放出する
- **emotion** 名 感情，感動
- **emotionally** 副 精神的に
- **empire** 名 帝国
- **end** 熟 at the end of ～の終わりに in the end とうとう，ついに
- **engineer** 名 技師
- **England** 名 イングランド，英国
- **enormous** 形 巨大な
- **enough** 熟 cannot ～ enough いくら～してもしたりない enough to do ～するのに十分な
- **enroll** 動 入学する
- **ensure** 動 保証する
- **entire** 形 全体の，完全な
- **entropy** 名 エントロピー《(社会や体系内で不可避に起きる)無秩序化，衰退》
- **equation** 名 方程式
- **escape** 動 逃げる，免れる
- **escort** 動 付き添う
- **essay** 名 随筆，エッセイ
- **essence** 名 本質，核心 in essence 要するに，突き詰めると
- **estimate** 動 見積もる
- **etc** 略 ～など，その他(= et cetera)
- **European** 形 ヨーロッパ(人)の
- **evaporate** 動 蒸発する，消えてなくなる
- **event horizon** 事象の地平線
- **eventually** 副 結局は，最終的には
- **ever** 熟 as ever 相変わらず，これまでのように as ～ as ever 相変わ

- らず~
- **everyone** 代誰でも、全員
- **everything** 代すべてのこと[もの]、何でも、何もかも theory of everything 万物の理論《電磁気力・弱い力・強い力・重力を統一的に記述する統一場理論》
- **everywhere** 副どこにでも
- **evidence** 名証拠
- **evolve** 動進化する
- **example** 熟 for example たとえば
- **except** 前~を除いて、~のほかは
- **excitedly** 副興奮して
- **excitement** 名興奮(すること)
- **exciting** 形興奮させる、わくわくさせる
- **execute** 動達成する、遂行する
- **exist** 動存在する、ある
- **expand** 動膨張する
- **expect** 動予期[予測]する
- **expense** 名出費、費用
- **experiment** 名実験 動実験する、試みる
- **experimental** 形実験の、試験的な experimental philosophy 実験哲学 experimental physics 実験物理学
- **expire** 動有効期限が切れる、終了する
- **explore** 動探検[調査]する、切り開く
- **explosion** 名爆発
- **expression** 名表現、表情
- **extra** 形追加の
- **extremely** 副非常に
- **ex-wife** 名前妻
- **eyeglasses** 名めがね

F

- **facial** 形顔の
- **fact** 熟 in fact 実際に(は)、それどころか
- **faculty** 名(大学の)学部、学科
- **fall** 熟 fall down 落ちる、転ぶ fall in love 恋におちる fall in love with ~と恋におちる fall into ~に陥る
- **fame** 名評判、名声
- **family dynamics** 家族の動態(ふれ合いなど)
- **farther** 副さらに進んで
- **fascinate** 動魅惑する、うっとりさせる
- **fast-growing** 形急成長の
- **favor** 熟 work in someone's favor ~に都合がいい形で機能する
- **fear** 動恐れる、心配する
- **feature** 動~を特集する
- **feeble** 形弱い
- **feed** 動食物を摂取する、食物を与える
- **feel like** ~のような感じがする
- **feeling** 名感じ、気持ち
- **fellow** 名①同僚 ②会員 Fellow of the Royal Society 王立学会特別研究員
- **fellowship** 名特別研究員の資格[地位・身分]、特別奨学金
- **Fermi National Accelerator Laboratory** フェルミ国立加速器研究所《米国エネルギー省の国立研究所》
- **feudalism** 名封建制度
- **fiancée** 名婚約者、フィアンセ《フランス語》
- **figure** 名姿、人物、象徴 international figure 国際的な有名人 動計算する figure out (原因などを)解明する

Word List

- **filled with** 《be –》~でいっぱいになる
- **finalize** 動 (交渉などに)決着をつける
- **financial** 形 金銭(上)の
- **find out** 調べる, 解明する
- **finding** 名《-s》調査結果
- **fine-tuned** 形 微調整された
- **firework** 名 花火
- **fit** 動 調和する, 一致する
- **flight** 名 飛ぶこと, 飛行
- **float** 動 浮く, 浮かぶ
- **fluid** 名 液体
- **fly to** ~まで飛行機で行く
- **focus** 動 (関心・注意を)集中させる
- **follow-up** 形 引き続いての
- **footstep** 名 足跡, 歩み
- **force** 名 力 動 強制する, 力ずくで~する, 余儀なく~させる
- **form** 名 形態, 型 動 形成する
- **formally** 副 形式的に
- **former** 形 前の, 以前の
- **formulation** 名 系統的論述, 公式化
- **fortune** 名 幸運
- **forward** 副 将来に look forward to ~を楽しみに待つ
- **foundation** 名 財団法人, 基金
- **Frank Hawking** フランク・ホーキング《人名。ホーキング博士の父親》
- **Franklin Institute** フランクリン協会《ベンジャミン・フランクリンの遺産をもとに設立された研究所》
- **Franklin Medal** フランクリン・メダル《フランクリン協会から個人に贈られる科学技術賞》
- **Fred Hoyle** フレッド・ホイル《人名。イギリスの天文学者, SF作家。1915-2001》
- **frequent** 形 ひんぱんな
- **friendly** 形 親しみのある, 心地よい
- **frighten** 動 驚かせる, びっくりさせる
- **from ~ to** ~から…まで, ~から~へと
- **frontier** 名 辺境, 未開拓分野
- **frustrate** 動 いらいらさせる
- **frustration** 名 落胆, 失意
- **fulfill** 動 (要求を)満たす
- **full-time** 名 常勤の, 専任の
- **Fundamental Physics Prize** 名 基礎物理学賞《優れた基礎研究の業績をあげた物理学者に与えられる賞》
- **funding** 名 資金提供
- **further** 形 その上の, なおいっそうの 副 その上に, もっと

G

- **gain** 動 増す
- **Galileo** 名 ガリレオ(・ガリレイ)《人名。イタリアの学者。近代物理学・観測天文学の父。1564-1642》
- **gap** 名 隔たり, 断絶
- **gather** 動 集まる
- **gathering** 名 集まり, 集会
- **general** 形 一般の, 普通の
  general public 一般人[大衆]
  general relativity 一般相対性理論
- **Geneva** 名 ジュネーブ《地名》
- **genius** 名 天才
- **geometry** 名 幾何学
- **George and the Big Bang** 『宇宙の誕生・ビッグバンへの旅』《邦題》
- **George Ellis** ジョージ・エリス《人名。南アフリカの宇宙物理学者, 数学者。1939-》

- **George's Secret Key to the Universe** 『宇宙への秘密の鍵』《邦題》
- **George's Cosmic Treasure Hunt** 『宇宙に秘められた謎』《邦題》
- **get** 熟 can't get enough of ～をいくら得ても充分でない get along 仲良くする get one's point across 言いたいことを伝える get out of ～から抜け出る、～から脱皮する get over 乗り越える get smaller 小さくなる get worse 悪化する
- **give birth** 出産する
- **give up** あきらめる、断念する
- **go** 熟 go by (時が)過ぎる、経過する go on ～し続ける go on a date (人と)デートする go on a trip 旅行する go on and on どんどん続ける go on to ～に移る、～へ進む go through (つらいことなど)を体験する
- **Gonville and Caius College** ゴンヴィル・アンド・キーズ・カレッジ《ケンブリッジ大学のカレッジの一つ》
- **govern** 動 支配する
- **graduate** 形 大学院の
- **grandparent** 名 祖父母
- **grant** 動 承諾する、(なるほどと)認める 名 助成金、補助金交付
- **gravitational** 形 重力の、引力の gravitational collapse 重力崩壊 gravitational physics 重力物理学
- **gravity** 名 重力、引力 Gravity Research Foundation 重力研究財団
- **grow up** 成長する、大人になる
- **gypsy** 名 ジプシー、ロマ族 gypsy caravan ジプシーのキャラバン(幌馬車、移動住宅)

H

- **hall** 名 公会堂、ホール
- **hand** 熟 on the other hand 一方、他方では
- **hand-held** 形 手で操作できる
- **handsome** 形 端正な(顔立ちの)
- **handwriting** 名 筆跡
- **happen to** ～に起こる
- **happily** 副 喜んで
- **hardship** 名 (耐えがたい)苦難、辛苦
- **harm** 動 傷つける
- **have** 熟 don't have to ～する必要はない should have done ～すべきだった(のにしなかった)《仮定法》
- **Hawking radiation** ホーキング放射《ブラックホールからの熱的な放射現象》
- **healthy** 形 健康な
- **height** 名 《the -》絶頂、真っ盛り
- **help** 熟 cannot help ～ing ～せずにはいられない help ～ with … …を～の面で手伝う
- **hire** 動 雇う
- **honeymoon** 名 新婚旅行 動 新婚旅行を過ごす
- **honor** 名 名誉、光栄
- **honorary** 形 名誉として与えられる honorary doctorate 名誉博士号
- **horizon** 熟 event horizon 事象の地平線
- **household** 名 家族、世帯
- **housing** 名 住宅供給、住居
- **how to** ～する方法
- **however** 接 けれども、だが
- **Hughes Medal** ヒューズ・メダル《英国王立協会が物理化学分野の業績に対して贈る賞》
- **humanity** 名 人類
- **humankind** 名 (種としての)人類、人間

WORD LIST

I

- **icon** 名 象徴的な人物
- **identify with** ～と一体感を持つ
- **if** 熟 as if あたかも～のように, まるで～みたいに ask ～ if ～に…かどうか尋ねる see if ～かどうかを確かめる wonder if ～ではないかと思う
- **ignore** 動 無視する
- **illness** 名 病気
- **imagination** 名 想像(力), 空想
- **immediate** 形 さっそくの, 即座の
- **importantly** 副 重要なことには
- **impression** 名 印象
- **improve** 動 改善する[させる]
- **improvement** 名 改良, 改善
- **incident** 名 出来事, 事件
- **include** 動 含む, 勘定に入れる
- **including** 前 ～を含めて, 込みで
- **income** 名 収入, 所得
- **increase** 動 増やす, 増える
- **incredible** 形 信じられない, すばらしい, とてつもない
- **indeed** 副 実際, 本当に
- **industry** 名 産業, 工業
- **infection** 名 (病気などの)感染
- **infinity** 名 無限
- **infrared** 形 赤外線の
- **initial** 形 最初の, 初めの
- **initially** 副 初めは
- **inject** 動 注射[注入]する
- **injury** 名 けが
- **inn** 名 宿屋
- **insert** 動 挿入する, 入れる
- **insist on** ～を強く主張する, 要求する
- **inspiring** 形 (人を)奮起させる, 刺激的な
- **instant** 形 すぐの, 即時の
- **instantly** 副 すぐに
- **instead of** ～の代わりに, ～をしないで
- **institute** 名 協会, 研究所
- **Institute of Astronomy** インスティテュート・オブ・アストロノミー《ケンブリッジ大学で最大の天文学研究センター》
- **institution** 名 協会, 公共団体
- **Intel Corporation** インテル《社名。米国に本社を置く半導体素子メーカー》
- **intellect** 名 知性, 知力
- **intelligent** 形 頭のよい, 聡明な
- **intensive care unit** 集中治療室
- **interestingly** 副 興味深いことに
- **interface** 名 人とコンピューターとを仲介する装置, インターフェース
- **interfere** 動 干渉する
- **interpret** 動 通訳する
- **interpretation** 名 通訳
- **intimate** 形 (事情などに)詳しい
- **introduction** 名 ①まえがき ②導入, 採用
- **invitation** 名 招待(状)
- **involve** 動 関与する, 巻き込む, かかわらせる
- **Isaac Newton** アイザック・ニュートン《人名。英国の物理学者, 数学者, 自然哲学者。1642-1727》
- **Isobel Hawking** イソベル・ホーキング《人名。ホーキング博士の母親》
- **issue** 名 問題, 論点
- **It is difficult for someone to** (人)が…するのは困難である
- **It takes someone ～ to** (人)が…するのに～(時間など)がかかる
- **itself** 代 それ自体, それ自身

J

- **Jane Wilde** ジェーン・ワイルド《人名。ホーキング博士の最初の妻》
- **Jim Hartle** ジェームス・ハートル《人名。米国の物理学者。1939-》
- **Jonathan Hellyer Jones** ジョナサン・ヘルヤー・ジョーンズ《人名。音楽家。ホーキング一家の友人で協力者》
- **joy** 名 喜び

K

- **keep at** ～を根気よく続ける
- **keep ~ private** ～を内密にしておく
- **knowledge** 名 知識, 理解, 学問
- **known as**《be -》～として知られている
- **known to**《be -》～することで知られている

L

- **laboratory** 名 研究所
- **lateral** 名 側部 amyotrophic lateral sclerosis 筋萎縮性側索硬化症
- **launch** 動 送り出す, 放つ
- **law** 名 (科学の)法則
- **least** 熟 at least 少なくとも
- **leave ~ behind** ～を置いて出発する
- **lecture** 名 講義, 公演
- **legally** 副 合法的に, 法律的に
- **Leonard Cheshire Foundation** レナード・チェシャー財団《障害者を支援する慈善団体》
- **leukemia** 名 白血病
- **level** 名 水準, 程度
- **lie** 動 (ある状態に)ある, 存在する
- **lifetime** 名 一生, 生涯
- **lift** 動 持ち上げる, 上がる
- **light cone** 光円錐《四次元空間において光の道筋を表す面》
- **like** 熟 feel like ～のような感じがする
- **limb** 名 手足, 四肢
- **lip** 名 唇
- **list** 名 名簿, 一覧表
- **live on** ～を糧として生きる
- **locate** 動 居住する
- **London** 名 ロンドン《英国の首都》
- **Long Melford** ロング・メルフォード《地名》
- **longer** 熟 no longer もはや～でない[～しない]
- **longtime** 形 昔からの
- **look back on** ～を回想する, 追憶する
- **look forward to** ～を楽しみに待つ, 期待する
- **look into** ～を調査する
- **loss** 名 喪失, 減損
- **Lou Gehrig** ルー・ゲーリッグ《人名。米国のプロ野球選手。1903-1941》 Lou Gehrig's disease ルー・ゲーリッグ病《筋萎縮性側索硬化症の別名》
- **love** 熟 fall in love 恋におちる fall in love with ～と恋におちる
- **lovely** 形 すばらしい
- **Lucasian Professor** ルーカシアン教授《ケンブリッジ大学の現職の数学教授に与えられる称号》
- **Lucy Hawking** ルーシー・ホーキング《人名。ホーキング博士の娘》

M

- **MacArthur Foundation** マッ

Word List

カーサー基金《米国に本部を置く慈善基金団体》
- **main** 形 主な, 主要な
- **mainstream** 形 主流の
- **major** 形 重要な, 主要な, 大幅な
- **make a speech** 演説をする
- **make a visit** 〜を訪問する
- **make the most of** 〜を最大限利用する
- **mammal** 名 哺乳類
- **mankind** 名 人類, 人間
- **marriage** 名 結婚(生活・式)
- **marry** 動 結婚する
- **Martin Rees** マーティン・リース《人名。英国の宇宙物理学者。1942-》
- **Mary Hawking** メアリー・ホーキング《人名。ホーキング博士の妹》
- **massive** 形 巨大な
- **master** 名 ①所有者, 主 ②校長
- **mathematical** 形 数学の, 数理的な
- **mathematically** 副 数学的に
- **mathematician** 名 数学者
- **mathematics** 名 数学
- **Maxwell Prize** マクスウェル賞《英国物理学会が理論物理学分野での業績を称えて贈る賞》
- **May Ball** メイボール《ケンブリッジ大学で年度末に行われる学生主催の舞踏会》
- **meaningful** 形 重要な, 意味を持つ
- **meanwhile** 副 それまでの間, 一方では
- **mechanics** 名 力学 quantum mechanics 量子力学
- **medal** 名 メダル, 勲章
- **media** 名 メディア, マスコミ
- **medical** 形 医学, 医療の
- **medication** 名 投薬, 薬による治療
- **meet with** 〜に出会う
- **memoir** 名 回顧録, 自叙伝
- **memorable** 形 記憶すべき, 忘れられない
- **memory** 名 記憶(力)
- **mentally** 副 精神的に
- **mercy** 名 慈悲, 幸運
- **messy** 形 ボサボサの
- **midair** 名 空中
- **mind** 名 心, 精神, 知性
- **Mini** 名 ミニ《イギリスのブリティッシュ・モーター・コーポレーション(BMC)社の大衆車》
- **miserable** 形 みじめな, 哀れな
- **mission** 名 使命, 任務
- **model** 名 模型, 理論
- **modern** 形 現代[近代]の
- **modern-day** 形 現代の
- **modify** 動 改造する
- **molecular** 形 分子の
- **molecule** 名 分子, 微粒子
- **moment** 名 瞬間, ちょっとの間
- **monitoring** 名 監視, モニタリング
- **monster** 名 怪物
- **mop** 名 モップ
- **more and more** ますます
- **more of** 〜よりもっと
- **more than** 〜以上
- **Moscow** 名 モスクワ《ロシアの首都》
- **most** 熟 make the most of 〜を最大限利用する
- **mostly** 副 ほとんど
- **motivation** 名 やる気, 動機
- **motor neuron disease** 運動ニューロン疾患
- **motor skill** 運動技能

- **motorized** 形 電動の
- **movement** 名 動き, 運動
- **much** 熟 as much as ～と同じだけ
- **much-needed** 形 切望していた
- **multiple sclerosis** 多発性硬化症
- **muscle** 名 筋肉, 筋力
- **mysterious** 形 不可解な

N

- **national** 形 国家[国民]の national pride 国家威信
- **nation-wide** 形 全国的な
- **necessarily** 副 ①必ず, 必然的に ②《not –》必ずしも～でない
- **Neil McKendrick** ニール・マッケンドリック《人名。ゴンヴィル・アンド・キーズ・カレッジの学長》
- **nerve** 名 神経
- **network** 名 人脈, ネットワーク
- **neurological** 形 神経学の
- **neuron** 名 神経細胞, ニューロン motor neuron disease 運動ニューロン疾患
- **New York** ニューヨーク《米国の都市;州》
- **newborn** 形 生まれたばかりの
- **news** 名 報道, ニュース, 知らせ
- **Newtonian** 形 ニュートンの Newtonian proportions ニュートンなみの重要さ, 偉大性
- **night** 熟 day and night 昼も夜も
- **nightly** 形 夜間の, 夜ごとの
- **no doubt** きっと, たぶん
- **no longer** もはや～でない[～しない]
- **no one** 誰も[一人も]～ない
- **Nobel Prize** ノーベル賞《ノーベル財団主催の「人類に最大の貢献をもたらした人々」へ贈られる賞》
- **nobody** 代 誰も[1人も]～ない
- **none** 代 (～の)誰も…ない
- **non-scientific** 形 非科学的な
- **normal** 形 標準的な
- **not always** 必ずしも～であるとは限らない
- **not only A but also B** Aのみならず B も
- **not yet** まだ～してない
- **note** 動 ①書き留める ②注意[注目]する
- **notice** 動 気づく, 認める
- **noticeably** 副 著しく
- **nuclear** 形 核の, 原子力の
- **nurse** 名 看護師[人]
- **nursing home** 介護施設
- **nutshell** 名 クルミの殻 in a nutshell 簡潔に言って

O

- **object** 名 物体
- **occasionally** 副 時折, 時たま
- **occur** 動 (事が)起こる, 生じる
- **of course** もちろん, 当然
- **offer** 動 申し出る, 提供する 名 申し出, 提供
- **officially** 副 正式に
- **on and on** 引き続き
- **one** 熟 no one 誰も[一人も]～ない one of ～の1つ[人]
- **onto** 前 ～の上へ[に]
- **opera** 名 オペラ
- **operate** 動 (機会などが)動く, 活動する
- **operation** 名 手術
- **opinionated** 形 自説を曲げない

WORD LIST

- **opportunity** 名 好機, チャンス
- **option** 名 選択(の余地), 選択可能物
- **organization** 名 組織, 団体, 機関
- **origin** 名 起源, 発端
- **original** 形 始めの, 元の, 本来の
- **other** 熟 each other お互いに on the other hand 一方, 他方では
- **outlive** 動 生き延びる, 長生きする
- **outsider** 名 よそ者, 部外者
- **outspoken** 形 率直な, 遠慮のない
- **overcome** 動 打ち勝つ, 克服する be overcome with ～に圧倒される
- **own** 熟 of one's own 自分自身の on one's own 自力で
- **Oxford** 名 オックスフォード《地名》
- **Oxford University** オックスフォード大学《英国で最も古い大学》

P

- **pack** 動 ～を満員にする
- **paid** 形 有給の
- **pajama** 名 《通例-s》パジャマ
- **parent** 名 《-s》両親
- **participate** 動 参加する, 加わる
- **particle** 名 粒子 particle physics 素粒子物理学
- **particular** 形 特有の
- **Pasadena** 名 パサディナ《地名》
- **pass by** ～のそばを通る[通り過ぎる]
- **path** 名 進路
- **patience** 名 忍耐(力)
- **patient** 名 病人, 患者
- **patron** 名 後援者
- **peaceful** 形 平和な, 穏やかな
- **per** 前 ～につき, ～ごとに

- **perfectly** 副 完全に, 申し分なく
- **perhaps** 副 たぶん, ことによると
- **period** 名 期間, 時代
- **permanent** 形 永久の
- **permanently** 副 恒久的に, 取り外せないように
- **personal** 形 個人の, 私的な
- **personality** 名 人格, 個性
- **perspective** 名 観点, 視点
- **Peter De'Ath** ピーター・デアト《人名。ホーキング博士が教えている学生》
- **PhD** 略 博士号 (= Doctor of Philosophy)
- **Philadelphia** 名 フィラデルフィア《地名》
- **Philippa Hawking** フィリッパ・ホーキング《人名。ホーキング博士の妹》
- **philosophical** 形 哲学の
- **philosophy** 名 哲学 experimental philosophy 実験哲学
- **photo** 名 写真
- **physical** 形 ①身体の, 肉体の ② 物理学の physical experiment 物理的実験
- **physically** 副 肉体的に
- **physicist** 名 物理学者
- **physics** 名 物理学 experimental physics 実験物理学 gravitational physics 重力物理学 particle physics 素粒子物理学 quantum physics 量子物理学 theoretical physics 理論物理学
- **place** 熟 take place 行われる
- **platform** 名 演壇
- **platonic** 形 純精神的な, プラトニックの
- **pleasant** 形 (物事が)楽しい, 心地よい
- **Plumian Professor** プルミアン

教授《ケンブリッジ大学の天文・実験物理学の教授の称号》
- **pneumonia** 名 肺炎
- **point** 名 a point in time 時点 get one's point across 言いたいことを伝える point of pride 誇りに関わること
- **Poland** 名 ポーランド《国名》
- **political** 形 政治の, 行政に関する
- **politics** 名 政治(学)
- **Pontifical Academy** ローマ教皇庁立科学アカデミー
- **Pope Pius XI Gold Medal** ピウス11世メダル《ローマ教皇庁立科学アカデミーが主催する, 45歳以下の功績ある科学者に贈られる賞》
- **popularity** 名 人気, 流行
- **popularize** 動 ～を世に広める
- **portray** 動 表現する, 描写する
- **position** 名 地位, 身分, 職
- **potential** 名 可能性, 潜在能力
- **pound** 名 ①ポンド《英国の通貨単位：記号£》②重量の単位, 約0.454kg
- **pregnant** 形 妊娠している
- **presentation** 名 概要説明, プレゼンテーション
- **preserve** 動 維持する
- **president** 名 ①大統領 ②総裁, 会長
- **Presidential Medal of Freedom** 大統領自由勲章《米国が文民に贈る最高位の勲章》
- **pressure** 名 重荷, プレッシャー
- **prestige** 名 名声, 威信
- **prestigious** 形 世評の高い, 名声のある
- **previous** 形 以前の
- **previously** 副 以前に[は]
- **pride** 名 誇り, 自慢 point of pride 誇りに関わること
- **principle** 名 原理, 原則 uncertainty principle 不確定性原理
- **priority** 名 優先すること
- **private** 形 非公開の, 内密の keep ～ private ～を内密にしておく
- **process** 名 ①経過, 進行 ②手順, 方法
- **professional** 形 専門の, プロの
- **professor** 名 教授 associate professor 准教授 Lucasian Professor ルーカシアン教授《ケンブリッジ大学の現職の数学教授に与えられる称号》Plumian Professor プルミアン教授《ケンブリッジ大学の天文学・実験物理学の教授の称号》
- **prognosis** 名 予後診断, 予測
- **progress** 名 進歩, 前進 動 進行する
- **progressive** 形 進歩的な
- **promote** 動 宣伝する
- **promotion** 名 昇進
- **properly** 副 適切に
- **property** 名 性質, 特性
- **proportions** 名 (物事の)重要度
- **propose** 動 ①結婚を申し込む ②～を提案する
- **protective of** ～に対して過保護な
- **prove** 動 証明する
- **provide** 動 供給する, 提供する
- **public** 名 一般の人々, 大衆 general public 一般人[大衆] 形 公共の
- **publication** 名 出版(物)
- **publicity** 名 宣伝, 広報
- **publish** 動 ①発表[公表]する ②出版[発行]する
- **publishable** 形 出版する価値がある
- **publisher** 名 出版社
- **pursue** 動 追求する, 従事する
- **put on** ①～を身につける, 着る ②(薬などを)処方する

Word List

- **put time or effort into** ～に時間や手間をかける

Q

- **quantum** 形 量子力学的な
  quantum mechanics 量子力学
  quantum physics 量子物理学
- **queen** 名 女王
- **quit** 動 やめる, 辞職する

R

- **radiate** 動 放射する, 発散する
- **radiation** 名 放射 Hawking radiation ホーキング放射《ブラックホールからの熱的な放射現象》
- **radio** 名 ラジオ
- **raid** 名 急襲 air raid 空襲, 空爆
- **raise** 動 上げる, 高める, ～を育てる
- **ramp** 名 傾斜路, スロープ
- **range** 名 範囲
- **rapid** 形 急激な
- **rare** 形 まれな, 珍しい
- **rather** 副 むしろ, かえって rather than ～よりむしろ
- **reach out to** ～と心を通わせる
- **reader** 名 准教授
- **ready to** 《be -》すぐに[いつでも]～できる, ～する構えで
- **realize** 動 気がつく, 悟る
- **reason for** ～の理由
- **recently** 副 近ごろ, 最近
- **recognize** 動 認識する
- **reconcile** 動 一致させる, 調和させる
- **reconnect** 動 ～と再び連絡を取る
- **record** 動 録音[録画]する
- **recover** 動 回復する
- **recovery** 名 回復
- **refuse** 動 拒絶する, 断る
- **regain** 動 取り戻す
- **regular** 形 定期的な
- **reject** 動 断る
- **relation** 名 関係
- **relationship** 名 人間関係
- **relativity** 名 相対性, 相対性原理 general relativity 一般相対性理論
- **relaxing** 形 くつろいだ
- **release** 動 (苦痛などから)解放する, 自由にする
- **relevant** 形 当該の
- **relief** 名 (苦痛・心配などの)除去, 軽減, 安心
- **remain** 動 (～の)ままである[いる]
- **remarkable** 形 注目に値する, すばらしい
- **renew** 動 更新する
- **renowned** 形 名声のある
- **replace** 動 取り替える, 差し替える
- **reply** 動 答える, 返事をする
- **reproduce** 動 再現する, 模造する
- **request** 名 願い, 要求(物)
- **require** 動 ①必要とする, 要する ②命じる
- **research** 名 調査, 研究 動 調査する, 研究する
- **resist** 動 抵抗[反抗・反撃]する
- **respect** 名 尊敬, 尊重 動 尊敬[尊重]する
- **respectively** 副 それぞれに
- **respond** 動 反応する
- **responsibility** 名 責任, 義務, 責務
- **result** 名 結果, 成り行き 動 (結果として)起こる result in 結果的に～をもたらす

- **retire** 動 退職[引退]する
- **reveal** 動 明らかにする, 暴露する
- **reverse** 動 覆す
- **review** 動 批評する, 検閲する
- **revolutionary** 形 画期的な, 革命的な
- **rewrite** 動 書き直す 名 書き直し(原稿)
- **rise to the challenge** 困難にうまく対処する
- **Robert George Hawking** ロバート・ジョージ・ホーキング《人名。ホーキング博士の息子》
- **rocket** 動 打ち上げる, 急発進させる
- **Roger Penrose** ロジャー・ペンローズ《英国の数学者, 宇宙物理学者。1931-》
- **role** 名 役割, 任務
- **romantic** 形 ロマンチックな
- **Rome** 名 ローマ《イタリアの首都》
- **rosy** 形 バラ色の
- **rotation** 名 交替, ローテーション
- **roughly** 副 おおよそ
- **routine** 名 お決まりの手順, 日課
- **row** 動 (ボートを)こぐ
- **rower** 名 ボートの漕ぎ手
- **royal** 形 王の, 国立の Royal Astronomical Society 王立天文学会, ロンドン天文学会 Royal Opera House 王立オペラ劇場 Royal Society 王立協会[学会]《英国にある世界最古の科学学会》
- **rule out** 除外する
- **rumor** 動 ~とうわさする
- **run out** 時間切れになる, 使い果たす
- **rush** 動 急行する
- **Russia** 名 ロシア《国名》
- **Russian** 名 ロシア(人)の

S

- **sacrifice** 名 犠牲
- **sadden** 動 ~を悲しませる
- **sadly** 副 不幸にも
- **salary** 名 給料
- **sale** 名 売上高
- **sample** 名 (分析のための)試料, 標本
- **satisfy** 動 満足させる
- **saving** 名《-s》貯金
- **scale** 名 規模, 程度, スケール
- **scientific** 形 科学の, 科学的な
- **sclerosis** 名 硬化(症) amyotrophic lateral sclerosis 筋萎縮性側索硬化症 multiple sclerosis 多発性硬化症
- **scream** 動 叫ぶ, 金切り声を出す
- **search** 熟 in search of ~を探し求めて
- **Seattle** 名 シアトル《地名》
- **security** 名 保証, 確保
- **see ~ as** ~を…と考える
- **see if** ~かどうかを確かめる
- **seem to be** ~であるように思われる
- **self-aware** 形 自意識過剰の
- **self-control** 名 自己抑制
- **seminar** 名 研究会, セミナー
- **sense** 名 ①感覚, 感じ ②意味 in a sense ある意味では
- **sensor** 名 感知装置, センサー
- **sentence** 名 文章
- **separate** 形 分かれた, 別々の
- **Serbo-Croatian** 名 セルビア・クロアチア語
- **series** 名 一続き, シリーズ
- **set a date** 日取りを決める
- **set to** 《be-》~することになっている

WORD LIST

- **set to work** 仕事に取り掛かる
- **shadow** 名影
- **shift** 名(交代制の)勤務(時間), シフト
- **shoelace** 名靴ひも
- **shortly** 副まもなく, すぐに
- **should have done** 〜すべきだった(のにしなかった)《仮定法》
- **show up** 顔を出す, 現れる
- **shrink** 動縮小する
- **shut down** (活動などを)停止する
- **shy** 形内気な, 恥ずかしがりの
- **significant** 形重要な, 有意義な
- **silence** 名沈黙, 静寂
- **similar to** 《be ‐》〜に似ている
- **simplify** 動簡単にする, 平易にする
- **simply** 副①単に, ただ ②断じて, どうしても
- **Simpsons** 名《The ‐》ザ・シンプソンズ《米国の長寿アニメ》
- **singularity** 名特異点 Singularities and the Geometry of Space-Time『特異点と時空の幾何学』
- **situation** 名状況, 境遇
- **skill** 名技能 motor skill 運動技能
- **slender** 形ほっそりとした
- **slurred** 形不明瞭な, ろれつが回らない
- **smaller** 熟 get smaller 小さくなる
- **small-scale** 形小規模の
- **so** 熟 and so それだから, それで so 〜 that … 非常に〜なので…
- **social** 形社会の, 社会的な
- **socialist** 名社会主義者, 社会党員
- **society** 名社会, 世間
- **software** 名コンピューターを機能させるためのプログラム, ソフト(ウェア)
- **solution** 名解答
- **solve** 動解く, 解決する
- **someone** 代ある人, 誰か
- **something** 代①ある物, 何か ②いくぶん, 多少
- **sometime** 副いつか, そのうち
- **sometimes** 副時々, 時たま
- **somewhat** 副いくらか, 多少
- **source** 名原因
- **space-time** 名時空
- **spark** 動火花を出す, 〜に拍車をかける
- **speak out** はっきり[遠慮なく]言う
- **speak to** 〜と話す
- **specialize** 動専門にする, 専攻する
- **speech** 熟 acceptance speech 受賞スピーチ, 就任演説 make a speech 演説をする
- **spine** 名背骨, 脊椎
- **split into** 〜に分かれる
- **sponsor** 動出資する, スポンサーになる
- **St. Albans** セントオールバンズ《地名》
- **stable** 形安定した, 堅固な
- **staff** 名職員, スタッフ
- **stair** 名《-s》階段
- **stance** 名立場
- **stand** 動〜に耐える, 我慢する
- **state** 名①あり様, 状態 ②(アメリカなどの)州 動述べる, 表明する
- **statement** 名声明, 述べること
- **status** 名(社会的な)地位, 立場
- **stay at** (場所)に泊まる
- **steady-state** 形定常状態の steady-state universe 定常宇宙

THE BIOGRAPHY OF STEPHEN HAWKING

- **Stephen William Hawking** スティーヴン・ウィリアム・ホーキング《人名。英国の理論物理学者。1942-》
- **stick** 名棒, スティック
- **stock market** 株式市場
- **stream** 名(一定の)流れ
- **strength** 名力, 強み
- **striking** 形印象的な, 魅力的な
- **strive** 動努める, 奮闘する
- **struck** 動 strike (襲う)の過去, 過去分詞
- **structure** 名構造
- **struggle** 動もがく, 奮闘する
- **stuck** 動 stick (貼る)の過去, 過去分詞
- **style** 名流儀, 様式
- **success** 名成功, 上首尾
- **successfully** 副首尾よく, うまく
- **such a** そのような
- **such as** たとえば〜, 〜のような
- **Sue Masey** スー・マッセイ《人名。ホーキング博士の助手》
- **suffer** 動 (病気などに)苦しむ, 悩む
- **Suffolk** 名サフォーク《地名》
- **suggest** 動 ①提案する ②示唆する
- **suitable** 形適当な, ふさわしい
- **sum up** 要約する, 総括する
- **summer school** 夏期講習会
- **support** 動養う, 援助する 名援助, 扶養
- **surface** 名表面
- **surgery** 名手術
- **surprisingly** 副驚いたことに, 意外にも
- **surround** 動取り巻く
- **surrounding** 名《-s》周囲の状況, 環境
- **survive** 動生き残る, 長生きする
- **suspect** 動疑う, (〜ではないかと)思う
- **swallow** 動飲み込む
- **swollen** 形腫れ上がった
- **symptom** 名兆候, 症状

T

- **tackle** 動 (問題などに)取り組む
- **take** 熟 It takes someone 〜 to … (人)が…するのに〜(時間など)がかかる take away 取り上げる, 奪い去る take care of 〜の世話をする, 〜の面倒を見る take off 取り去る, 〜を取り除く take place 行われる take up (仕事などを)引き受ける, 担う take 〜 out 〜を取り除く take 〜 to … 〜を…に連れて行く
- **taxi** 名タクシー
- **technology** 名科学技術, テクノロジー
- **television** 名テレビ
- **tell 〜 to** 〜に…するように言う
- **temper** 名気質, 気性
- **tension** 名緊張(関係)
- **term** 名 ①期間, 期限 ②《-s》関係, 仲 on 〜 terms with … …と〜な仲である
- **than** 熟 more than 〜以上 rather than 〜よりむしろ
- **thankfully** 副ありがたいことに
- **theatre** 名劇場
- **theoretical physicist** 理論物理学者
- **theoretical physics** 理論物理学
- **theory** 名理論, 学説 theory of everything 万物の理論《電磁気力・弱い力・強い力・重力を統一的に記述する統一場理論》

Word List

- **there is no way** ～する見込みはない
- **thermodynamics** 名 熱力学
- **thesis** 名 (学位)論文
- **thick** 形 厚い
- **thinker** 名 思想家
- **those who** ～する人々
- **threat** 名 脅かすもの
- **threaten** 動 脅かす
- **three-story** 形 三階建ての
- **thrill** 動 わくわくする[させる]
- **throat** 名 のど, 気管
- **throughout** 前 ～中, ～を通じて
- **throw a party** パーティーを開く
- **throw off** (人を)うろたえさせる, 混乱させる
- **thus** 副 このようにして
- **tick** 動 カチカチと時を刻む **as the minutes ticked by** 時が刻々と過ぎる中で
- **Tim** 名 ティム《ティモシーの愛称》
- **time** 熟 **a point in time** 時点 **any time** いつでも **at the time** そのころ, 当時は **by the time of** ～の時までに **by this time** この時までに, もうすでに **each time** ～するたびに **put time or effort into** ～に時間や手間をかける
- **Timothy Hawking** ティモシー・ホーキング《人名。ホーキング博士の息子》
- **title** 名 題名, タイトル
- **topic** 名 話題, 主題
- **total** 形 完全な 名 全体, 合計
- **tour** 名 巡業, ツアー 動 (観光)旅行する
- **tracheotomy** 名 気管切開術
- **translate** 動 翻訳する, 訳す
- **transportation** 名 交通(機関), 輸送手段
- **treasure** 名 財宝, 宝物
- **treat** 動 扱う, 取り扱う
- **Trinity College** トリニティ・カレッジ《ケンブリッジ大学を構成するカレッジの一つ》
- **Trinity Hall** トリニティ・ホール《ケンブリッジ大学を構成する大学の一つ》
- **trip** 熟 **go on a trip** 旅行する
- **triumph** 名 (大)勝利, 大成功
- **tropical disease** 熱帯病
- **truly** 副 全く, 本当に
- **truth** 名 事実, 真実
- **tube** 名 管, 筒
- **tudor-style** 形 チューダー様式の《16世紀イギリスの建築・装飾様式》
- **turn** 熟 **at the turn of the century** 世紀の変わり目に **turn out to be** ～という結果になる **turn to** ～を始める

U

- **UK** 名 英国, イギリス(=United Kingdom)
- **uncertainty principle** 不確定性原理
- **unconscious** 形 意識不明の
- **undergo** 動 経験する, 耐える
- **undergraduate** 形 学部の学生の
- **undone** 動 undo(ほどく)の過去分詞
- **undress** 動 衣服を脱ぐ
- **unhappy** 形 不幸な
- **unify** 動 一つにする, 統一する
- **unique** 形 唯一の, ユニークな, 独自の
- **unit** 名 部署, ユニット **intensive care unit** 集中治療室

- **United States** 名 アメリカ合衆国《国名》
- **universe** 名《the ~/the U-》宇宙, 全世界　steady-state universe 定常宇宙　The Universe in a nutshell『ホーキング, 未来を語る』《邦題》
- **University of Cambridge** ケンブリッジ大学《英国の総合大学》
- **University of Maryland** メリーランド大学《米国の州立総合大学》
- **unpleasant** 形 不愉快な, いやな
- **unsolved** 形 未解決の
- **unstoppable** 形 止められない
- **untiring** 形 疲れ知らずの
- **up until** ～まで
- **update** 動 ～を更新する, 改訂する
- **uphold** 動 支持する, 掲げる
- **urge** 動《~ … to ~》…に～するよう心に勧める

V

- **vacuum** 名 吸い込むこと, 真空
- **valid** 形 正当な, 妥当な
- **valuable** 形 有益な, 重要な
- **value** 動 ～を評価する, 大切にする
- **Vanity Fair** ヴァニティフェア《雑誌名》
- **various** 形 変化に富んだ, さまざまの, たくさんの
- **vast** 形 ばく大な
- **Vatican** 名 バチカン《市国》《地名》
- **verbally abuse** 口汚くののしる
- **vibrant** 形 力強い, 生き生きとした
- **vice** 形 代理の, 副～
- **victim** 名 犠牲者, 被害者
- **violent** 形 暴力的な
- **visit** 熟 make a visit to ～を訪問する
- **visitor** 名 訪問客
- **visualize** 動 思い浮かべる, 心に描く
- **vocal** 形 主張する, 強く求める
- **vote** 名 投票, 票決 動 投票する

W

- **Washington** 名 ワシントン《米国の首都；州》
- **way** 熟 in a way ある意味では　in this way このようにして　there is no way ～する見込みはない　way of ～する方法　way to ～する方法
- **weaken** 動 弱くなる
- **weakness** 名 弱さ, 弱点
- **wealth** 名 富, 財産
- **wealthy** 形 裕福な, 金持ちの
- **wed** 動 結婚させる, 結婚する
- **weigh** 動 重さが～ある
- **weightless** 形 重量のない
- **well** 熟 as well なお, その上, 同様に　as well as ～と同様に, ～だけでなく…も
- **well-known** 形 よく知られた, 有名な
- **well-read** 形 よく読まれている
- **Werner Israel** ウェルナー・イスラエル《人名。カナダの物理学者。1931–》
- **Westfield College** ウェストフィールド・カレッジ《英国の州立大学》
- **whatever** 形 どんな～でも
- **wheelchair** 名 車いす
- **whereas** 接 ～であるのに対して
- **while** 熟 for a while しばらくの間
- **who** 熟 those who ～する人々
- **whoever** 代 ～する人は誰でも
- **whole** 形 全体の, すべての
- **wide** 形 幅の広い, 広範囲の

Word List

W

- **witness** 動 目撃する
- **wonder** 動 不思議に思う，(〜かしらと)思う wonder if 〜ではないかと思う
- **work** 熟 set to work 仕事に取り掛かる work in 〜の分野で働く，〜に入り込む work in someone's favor 〜に都合がいい形で機能する work on 〜に取り組む，〜に従事する work out (問題を)解く，考え出す，答えが出る
- **world-famous** 形 世界的に有名な
- **worldwide** 形 世界的な，世界規模の
- **worry about** 〜のことを心配する
- **worse** 熟 get worse 悪化する
- **worst** 名《the -》最悪の事態
- **wrist** 名 手首
- **write to** 〜に手紙を書く

X

- **X-ray** 名《-s》X線，レントゲン

Y

- **Yakov Borisovich Zel'dovich** ヤーコフ・ボリソヴィチ・ゼルドヴィチ《人名。旧ソビエトの物理学者。1914-1987》
- **yearlong** 形 一年間に及ぶ
- **years** 熟 for years 何年も for 〜 years 〜年間，〜年にわたって
- **yet** 熟 not yet まだ〜してない yet another さらにもう一つの yet to いまだ〜されない
- **youngster** 名 少年，子ども
- **youth** 名 青春時代

Z

- **Zero Gravity Corporation** ゼロ・グラヴィティ・コーポレーション《会社名》
- **zero-gravity** 形 無重力状態の

English Conversational Ability Test
国際英語会話能力検定

● E-CATとは…
英語が話せるようになるためのテストです。インターネットベースで、30分であなたの発話力をチェックします。

www.ecatexam.com

● iTEP®とは…
世界各国の企業、政府機関、アメリカの大学300校以上が、英語能力判定テストとして採用。オンラインによる90分のテストで文法、リーディング、リスニング、ライティング、スピーキングの5技能をスコア化。iTEP®は、留学、就職、海外赴任などに必要な、世界に通用する英語力を総合的に評価する画期的なテストです。

www.itepexamjapan.com

ラダーシリーズ

The Biography of Stephen Hawking
スティーヴン・ホーキング・ストーリー

2016年6月5日　第1刷発行
2025年6月2日　第2刷発行

著　者　ニーナ・ウェグナー

発行者　賀川　洋

発行所　IBCパブリッシング株式会社
　　　　〒162-0804 東京都新宿区中里町29番3号
　　　　菱秀神楽坂ビル
　　　　Tel. 03-3513-4511　Fax. 03-3513-4512
　　　　www.ibcpub.co.jp

© IBC Publishing. Inc. 2016

印刷　株式会社シナノパブリッシングプレス
装丁　伊藤 理恵
組版データ　Sabon Roman + Georgia Bold

落丁本・乱丁本は、小社宛にお送りください。送料小社負担にてお取り替えいたします。本書の無断複写 (コピー) は著作権法上での例外を除き禁じられています。

Printed in Japan
ISBN978-4-7946-0414-9

[photo credit]
カバー　　Polaris/amanaimages
p.7　　　 Horst Friedrichs/Anzenberger/amanaimages
p.31, 71　Polaris/amanaimages
p.64　　　ZUMA Press/amanaimages